The day our daughter arrived, life changed for George and Marilyn McGinnis as it had never changed before. The carefree life-style of a couple who could invite friends over (or be invited) on a whim, go out for a pizza at midnight, read or type manuscripts for two hours uninterrupted came to a screeching halt.

The anticipation of parenthood gave way rather quickly to the realities of parenthood.

When she was hungry, she was hungry. It never occurred to her that *we* might be hungry, tired, busy or anything else. She wanted to be fed RIGHT NOW!

When she was wet (or worse), she was wet. And she wanted to be changed. NOW! Not whenever Mom or Dad got around to it.

If she decided that 3:00 A.M. was playtime, then it was playtime. Neither bottles, nor pacifiers, nor logical reasoning could convince her otherwise. She was in charge.

Twenty-two months later our once carefree life-style was pushed even further into never-never land. On a July summer evening our two baby boys arrived, one right after the other. We thought we were busy with one! With three there was no hope. If I stopped to go to the bathroom, I got behind.

To
Shana, Reed, Scott
who fill our lives with incredible joy
and
To
Hazel
who loves us

Give Me a Child Until He's Two
(then you take him until he's four!)

A Survival Guide for
Parents of Preschoolers

Marilyn McGinnis

Regal
Books
A Division of G/L Publications
Ventura, CA U.S.A.

Other good reading:
Good Times for Your Family by Wayne E. Rickerson
Too Big to Spank by Jay Kesler

The foreign language publishing of all Regal books is under the direction of GLINT. GLINT provides financial and technical help for the adaptation, translation and publishing of books in more than 85 languages for millions of people worldwide.

For more information write: GLINT, P.O. Box 6688, Ventura, California 93006

Published by Regal Books
A Division of GL Publications
Ventura, California 93006
Printed in U.S.A.

Library of Congress Catalog Card No. 80-54005
ISBN 0-8307-0785-9

Portions of this book originally appeared in *American Baby* and *Family Life Today* magazines.

Contents

Nine years ago my husband and I embarked on the great career of marriage. We were not teenagers, barely dry behind the ears. On the contrary, I was 32, George was 41. We had long since established ourselves in our careers. We had experienced the single scene long enough to know what we were looking for in a mate.

Two years after our marriage our first child, a son, was stillborn. Fourteen months later our daughter arrived. Twenty-two months later (almost three years to the day after the loss of our son), God blessed our home with *two* baby boys. We have known both the joys and the sorrows of parenting.

Parenting is unlike any other occupation in the world. We never really anticipate its challenges. Its joys are different from any we experience elsewhere. In a part of this book I have attempted to discuss as realistically as possible the adjustments we must make in order to fully enjoy our children.

There is no one easy way to parent preschoolers. Each child is different, and so are his parents. The suggestions in this book are ideas that have worked for us and for other parents. From these ideas you can pick and choose those that are most helpful to you.

I am not an expert on how to raise preschoolers. But I am a mother, who, at one point, had three children under the age of two. Now our daughter is six, our sons are four. I am still a mother of preschoolers.

This book has been written over a three-year-period. If I refer to my children as age two in one chapter, age four in another, and age three in yet another, do not think we have three sets of children! I prefer to leave their ages as they were at the time that particular sequence was written.

There is an inherent danger in writing this kind of book. The danger is that someday my children may read it and say, "Why didn't you try all those neat ideas, Mom?" Or, worse yet, "So much for all your wonderful suggestions, Mom, they didn't work." I leave that risk with the Lord.

I am deeply indebted to the moms and dads who took time from their busy lives with preschoolers to help me with this book, especially: Kyle, Pam, Craig and Lyne, Connie, Diane, Nancy, Tobi, Phillip and Cindy, John, Ralph, Kathy, and Audrey. Edna Burow and Alice Schrage read and evaluated the manuscript from the perspective of mothers whose children have passed the preschool years. Margaret Self, former managing editor of the Children's Division at Gospel Light Publications, gave the book a careful editing. Without my husband's help, there would be no book. Because of the kind of father he is, my job as a mother is much easier.

My prayer is that this book will help you strengthen the ties between you and your children, and between yourselves as parents, as together you guide your little ones through the preschool years.

PART I

GETTING YOURSELF TOGETHER AS A NEW PARENT

CHAPTER 1

You were
expecting roses?

The birth of our daughter occurred two weeks after the publication of my first book. To commemorate the book's debut, the publisher sent me an enormous bouquet of red roses. For days their beauty filled the dining area of our tiny duplex. My husband and I smelled their sweet fragrance, admired the rich red color, and rejoiced at the impending birth of our child.

Quite frankly, I haven't seen a rose since.

The day our daughter arrived, life changed for George and Marilyn McGinnis as it had never changed before. The carefree life-style of a couple who could invite friends over (or be invited) on a whim, go out for pizza at midnight, read or type manuscripts for two hours uninterrupted came to a screeching halt.

The anticipation of parenthood gave way rather quickly to the realities of parenthood.

When she was hungry, she was hungry. It never occurred to her that *we* might be hungry, tired, busy or anything else. She wanted to be fed RIGHT NOW!

When she was wet (or worse), she was wet. And she wanted to be changed. NOW! Not whenever Mom or Dad got around to it.

If she decided that 3:00 A.M. was playtime, then it was playtime. Neither bottles, nor pacifiers, nor logical reasoning could convince her otherwise. She was in charge.

Twenty-two months later our once carefree life-style was pushed even further into never-never land. On a July summer evening our two baby boys arrived, one right after the other. We thought we were busy with one! With three there was no hope. If I stopped to go to the bathroom, I got behind.

For the next 20 years (God willing there are no *further* additions to this family) our lives by choice and by necessity revolve around the three children He has entrusted to our care.

Gone (for awhile) is adult entertaining. Spilled food, childish chatter, and squabbles over who got the Bozo clown place mat are all in a parent's day. But such occurrences are hardly the fare to which outsiders should have to be subjected.

Gone are most of the spur of the moment pleasures. Especially if the baby-sitter has to be booked a year in advance.

Gone is uninterrupted *anything*. To be a mother is never to finish a sentence—or the dishes. In the few brief moments I have been sitting here typing, both boys (now age three) have brought me a hilarious report of how "Daddy carried us both in one towel (from the bathtub) to the bedroom!" and one boy showed me his pajama dilemma (also considered highly amusing)—bottoms on, tops rolled hopelessly around his chest, neck stretched completely out of shape.

An *hour* of solitude has been replaced by a *moment* of solitude—eagerly sought, quickly recognized, and cherished as if it were to last a lifetime.

Some days, in a mixture of humor and despair, I ask of whoever happens to be listening, "Now why was it I wanted to have children?" I'll tell you why I have children.

Because, despite all the hard work and frustration, children add a fullness and richness to life that can never be found anywhere else. Holding your own child in your arms and realizing that this tiny helpless infant is bone of your bone and flesh of your (and your mate's) flesh produces a bond of togetherness that only the Creator could bestow. It is the fulfillment of a lifetime. It simply was meant to be.

Because I like being a family. The hardest thing about being single was not belonging to anybody. My parents lived several hundred miles away and there were no relatives nearby to whom I was close. The loneliness of those years was often filled in part by—a family. A wonderful family of five who took me in whenever I needed to be taken, and made me feel like one of them. I like being part of a family. That, too, was meant to be.

Because I told God when I was very young that I didn't want an easy life. I want to grow in my Christian experience and come ever closer to Him. What better tool can God use to accomplish that goal than through the trials and tribulations of parenting? The onslaught of motherhood has taught me a lot about my-self—some good, some bad. Getting along as a family is where the rubber meets the road.

The transition from "married" to parenthood is a joyous one. But it is not easy. As I talk with other parents of preschool-ers, I find a goodly number of adjustments in thinking and in doing that parents must make when the children begin to arrive.

Some of the adjustments are happy ones.

"Becoming a mother was much better, more joyful and fulfilling than I expected."

"It's nice to have another person to love you, especially when the baby first begins responding to you. I love watching babies grow up."

"When they first begin to respond to you, you really appreci-ate being a parent."

"Having children taught us more about God's love for us. He must have some of the same feelings about us that we have for our children."

"Becoming a mother was the accomplishment of a life goal."

"The unexpected things kids do and say are so special."

"I love watching the beginning of their spiritual relationships, their unshakable faith in God."

Children are rewarding, fulfilling, the challenge of a lifetime.

Some of the adjustments of parenthood, however, are dif-ficult. Before the first child is born there are apprehensions. I wonder how I'll do as a parent? Will I know what to do with such a tiny creature? What will I do the first time he gets sick?

Will I love the baby? How do I know I've got a maternal/paternal instinct when I've never experienced it?

There are apprehensions about our mates. "I really wondered how my husband would do as a father," says my friend Eleanor. "He was very happy with just the two of us. He thought it was fun without children."

Once their daughter arrived, however, her apprehensions faded. Her husband adored their daughter. "Now," she says happily, "he wonders what on earth life would be like without Brenda."

And, of course, there are apprehensions about the child to be born. Will he/she be healthy? What if he has Down's syndrome, or is deformed, or sickly? Would we know how to cope?

Once the child arrives, the apprehensions begin to fade. In their place come a whole new set of adjustments.

None of us is fully prepared for the amount of time it takes to be a parent. In theory I knew that babies took a lot of time. But until our daughter arrived I had never experienced it. And it took awhile for it to sink in. I naively thought that life could go on pretty much as usual.

When Shana was about five months old and I was at wit's end trying to finish editing a book manuscript, it finally penetrated my thick skull that I could no longer keep up the writing/editing schedule I had set for myself. It was certainly not necessary for me to give it up entirely. But I would best keep my sanity and our household running smoothly if, until my daughter was older, I wrote only at my own pace and accepted no assignments that had immediate deadlines.

There are too many variables with small children to box yourself in. An editor doesn't really care that I had to sit up all night with a croupy kid. What he really cares about is that I said I'd have the manuscript to him by Friday and I blew it.

Within a few days after baby's arrival you begin to realize your loss of freedom, that feeling of being tied down. No longer can you pick up and go at the slightest whim to shop, visit a friend, or have a romantic dinner out with your husband. Suddenly you are a slave to the demands of a very tiny human being who controls your every action.

How well I recall the morning it took three hours to get my two babies and one toddler ready for an outing. By the time I got each one fed, changed and dressed, somebody had spit up, wet, messed his/her pants, or needed another bottle and it was time to start all over again! A far cry from the days when I simply picked up my purse, jumped into the car and left.

"I liked having my own schedule," says one mother, "not someone else's."

Dad used to go out with the "boys" one or two nights a week. Now he is housebound more often than he'd like—feeding babies, or watching the baby while his wife goes out to regain her sanity.

You must also adjust to the limited amount of time you can spend together as husband and wife. Your husband had a meeting at work that he really wants to discuss with you. But that's when the baby starts screaming with colic.

You reach lovingly for each other in the middle of the night, only to discover the warm body of your toddler lodged comfortably between you. You don't even know what hour of the night he climbed in.

You're dying to discuss some current event but the children are bubbling with news about *their* day's events. Before children you rarely had to plan time together. Now it becomes a necessity.

You must also adjust your expectations of how you, your mate, and your children will react in the real-life situations of family life. Before I had children I was such a quiet soul, even quite shy in my younger years. Since becoming a parent I have been transformed, at times, into a raving maniac. I never saw that side of myself before—and neither did my husband! He is a rather mild-mannered man himself, but there are days when the children push his back to the wall as well.

I will never scream at my children, I said (before I had any). That was before I discovered that children are born deaf, hard of hearing or, at best, practice selective listening. When the vibrations from a good scream have captured their attention, then you can speak to them in a normal tone of voice. But it's "not my nature" to scream.

As parents we must also deal with newfound feelings of hate and resentment. What? Hate my child? Yes, there are times when we do (for the moment). We resent the amount of time the children encroach on our freedom.

Sometimes those feelings of resentment are directed toward our spouse.

"You haven't changed his diaper in five days. Couldn't you do that one little thing to help?"

"I told you I had to go back to work tonight for a meeting. Surely you had time to at least heat up a can of stew so dinner would be ready."

The mark of maturity is not that we have those feelings, but in how we deal with them.

Another adjustment comes when we try to correlate what we've been "taught" about raising children with life as it really is.

One of the first things I did when I became a parent was to throw out just about everything I had ever learned concerning child rearing. A few sound principles do remain lodged in my cranium because I have proven them to be true. But a lot of theory written by people who probably never had children just doesn't cut it. Neither does some of the advice offered by well-meaning relatives and friends. Parenthood is a course each of us plows for himself.

As we struggle for a realistic approach to child rearing, *we make adjustments in our expectations of what we will do as parents and what our children will do and be.*

How did you *think* you would handle a particular situation? How did you *actually* handle it?

My children will never be seen at Sunday School or the supermarket in clothes that do not match, I said. That was before I learned that an important part of a preschooler's development is allowing him to make choices. Now, honestly, do maroon sox, green plaid shorts, and an orange and blue Star Trek shirt really look all that bad?

I will never let TV be a baby-sitter, I said. Dear God, if "Sesame Street" doesn't come on pretty soon I don't think I'll make it through dinner.

My children will never be seen in the front yard in their

underwear, I said. After five changes of clothes today, I'm just glad their bodies are covered.

I have learned that to expect a two-year-old to eat an already peeled banana or one that has been cut in half is to court disaster. (The "I'd rather do it myself" bit starts much earlier than I anticipated.) If the banana should happen to break in his hand, God forbid, a toothpick must be secured to put it back together. The first bite will take care of his tonsils.

I have learned that, contrary to popular opinion, a toddler can climb a 20-foot ladder to the roof with great dexterity and without falling to her death on the patio. The only damage is in the coronary suffered by her father.

I have also learned that the house will not be condemned for negligent upkeep when my two-year-olds rip their wallpaper from floor to ceiling. The hoarse throats suffered by the screaming parents is far more serious than the unkempt appearance of the boys' room.

With three children under the age of two, *I faced a serious adjustment in accepting my own limitations.* I used to be so self-sufficient. There wasn't much I couldn't handle myself. Suddenly I'm dissolving in tears at the slightest provocation from overwork, lack of sleep and an around-the-clock feeding schedule. Even with a lot of help from my husband, he still had to go to work (or we wouldn't eat) and he most assuredly had to get a reasonable amount of sleep at night (or he wouldn't be *able* to go to work). The solution, of course, was to hire help.

Hire help? Me? But I've always done my own housework. I've always taken care of the children myself. Another adjustment which, like any, has its own rewards. "Help" turned out to be a wonderful lady who has enriched our lives a thousand times over; also out-of-state grandparents who lighten the load considerably with their several-times-a-year visits.

During the first year with our boys I learned to *accept* help, as well as to give it. That, for me, was a valuable lesson.

For the woman who chooses to stay at home with her children and not work, a new adjustment comes almost immediately.

When I called Kyle, mother of five-month-old twin girls, to

interview her for this chapter, she was delighted. Yes, she could go out for coffee with me *tonight.*

"I'm at the stage where I'm really *missing the stimulation of adult conversation,* of having people around," she confided.

"Would you read this chapter for me when I get the first draft done?" I asked.

"Yes," she quickly replied. "It will keep my mind working."

Once you read voraciously, watched the news every night, talked about intellectual things with your husband. Now when he comes home, the highlight of the day is how often the baby spit up and the problems you're having with the diaper service.

For those who choose to go back to work after the baby is born, there is another set of adjustments. Should I really be working, or should I be at home with my child? The emphasis of women's lib that says you SHOULD be out working causes many ambivalent feelings.

If you have reconciled yourself to the working world, there may be a problem fusing your two personalities. "There's Pam, the nurse," says a mother of two, "in charge of a floor. And there's Pam, the mother, who gets little sleep, changes a lot of diapers and does a lot of things that are really rather boring."

Normal adjustments are intensified for single parents and women whose husbands work long hours, travel a lot, or disassociate themselves for one reason or another from care of the baby. Instead of the teamwork they had hoped for, they find themselves shouldering most of the responsibility alone.

"My husband was the youngest child," says one mother, "and was never around babies. He had no idea how to be a father. He used to tell me that taking care of the baby was my job because I was trained for it. By the time the second child arrived he helped more because he felt more adequate."

Some mothers are just as ill prepared to take care of a baby. And even if they're prepared "academically," it's not the same as experiencing it.

My friend Lyne is a nurse and teaches prepared childbirth classes. Yet after the birth of her first child she recalls, "When my mother left I remember looking into the crib and thinking, if I don't feed this child he will die."

"I took care of two much younger brothers and a sister when I was young," says another mother, "and besides that I'm a nurse. But I was totally unprepared for the 24-hour responsibility of being a mother."

An overwhelming sense of responsibility may hit whether you are well prepared or not. How many times I have looked at my children and thought, "What if I do my best and yet this child grows up to be a drug addict, or has an illegitimate child, or. . .?" Those are the times it is especially comforting to know that God is in control.

Just when you think *you're beginning to get the hang of parenthood, along comes the second child (or third, or?)*. And all your carefully thought-out ways of doing things are dashed to the winds. Because, in all likelihood, the next child will have a completely different personality from the first.

I knew the most about child-rearing when I had only one. My friend's two-year-old wouldn't stay in her bed at night. She would often be found sleeping on the floor in front of the heater or under the dining room table. *My* daughter never did that. Children should stay in their beds. And if they don't it's because the parents are too permissive, or too something.

Then along came our boys. The day they turned two they looked at the calendar and said to themselves, "Now's our chance." And for the next year or better neither rain, hail, sleet nor threats of annihilation at the hands of their parents would keep them in their beds. I learned how little I knew.

Each child added to the family brings added joy—and added tension—in any family situation. Occasionally we are able to spend time alone with just one of our children. Almost without exception, as soon as we have that child alone to ourselves, life suddenly becomes serene. Gone is the bickering over who wore the Superman pajamas last night and whose turn it is to pick up the toys in the living room. The "only" child has no one to fight with and has no need to compete for Mom and Dad's attention. He/she is a different child—and we are different parents.

I don't for a moment regret having three children. But I also recognize that the more little ones you add to your home, the more opportunity there is for tension. The psalmist advised,

"How good and how pleasant it is for brothers to live harmoniously together!" (Ps. 133:1). What he doesn't say is how long it takes to produce that happy cohabitation.

With the responsibility of parenthood comes the underlying fear of what we would do if we truly had to go it alone.

"Sometimes I have really scary feelings," says a mother of three. "My husband has had a lot of medical problems and I wonder what I'd do if something happened to him. I don't think I could support us."

Only briefly have we touched on the kinds of adjustments that come with parenthood. In the following chapters we will talk in more detail about the joys and frustrations of becoming a parent. To begin with, let's take a look at parenting from the masculine point of view, to see what it's like to be a father.

CHAPTER 2

It's Dad's
first child, too

I n her book *People in Process*, Maxine Hancock tells about
the adjustments she and her husband experienced with the
birth of their first child. The joys of becoming a new parent
soon gave way to intense pressures. As the tensions increased
words became sharp between them. She felt as if her husband
had no understanding at all of what she was going through.
Finally things reached a point where the only solution was to
talk.

> "Cam," I said, "I love you very much. You were
> wonderful to me while I was pregnant. But now I am
> finding you critical and unsympathetic. And this is a
> time when I just can't take it. I want to tell you some-
> thing. You are a man. And you don't know one little
> thing about what it takes to bear a child. A person
> cannot be stretched to the absolute limits of elasticity—
> physically and emotionally—and just go *snap!* right
> back into shape. You seem to think I should be able to
> pick up where I left off before I got pregnant. I'm telling
> you that I can't. I don't know what's wrong. I don't
> know if it's normal. But I'm telling you—it's *me*. I need
> your help now—not your criticism."

Cam listened carefully, then reached his hands across the table and placed them over mine. "I didn't know," he said. "I'm sorry." He paused, then went on. "But I think you need to be a bit more understanding, too."

I looked at him sharply, stiffening defensively.

Cam went on. "You've got to remember something, Maxine. *This is my first baby, too.*"[1]

No husband can fully understand the emotional and physical stretching a woman experiences when she becomes a mother. But neither can a woman understand what it feels like to be a father—unless her husband tells her.

Rather than try to tell you how I *think* fathers feel, I asked four fathers of preschool children to tell you themselves.

Paul was 23 when he and Sue had their first child. Their son is now four. Another child is on the way.

Glenn was well established in business when he married Annette at age 31. Five years later their first child—a daughter— was born. They now have two daughters, ages five and three. Glenn started a new career after his daughters were born.

Cliff and his wife Carol have a six-year-old son and a three-year-old daughter. He was 26 when his son was born. Cliff and Carol had been married two years.

At the age of 27 Mike married Lynae, a widow with two sons ages eight and two-and-a-half. Two years later their daughter was born. Mike has legally adopted his wife's two boys. Their daughter is not yet two. Mike serves on the staff of a large church.

How did you feel when your first child was born? Were there any surprises?

Paul: I was upset. I felt like I was too young to have a child. We had been married about a year, just out of college, and we had made a lot of plans. I was going to work and put my wife through school. Then I was going to go to seminary and she was going to support me.

Our first child was just not planned at all. It

cut into my priorities. It wasn't until close to the time James was born that I really began to resolve those deep-seated feelings. Actually, having a child was more life-changing than getting married. I didn't really realize the time commitment that is involved.

Glenn: I was 31 when I was married. We waited for five years to have a baby and Tracy was very much planned. We went to the Red Cross and Lamaze classes and were excited about having a child. The surprise was: It was an exhausting, exhilarating, somewhat frightening experience because of my concern for Annette and the baby in those last moments of a difficult birth. We learned all the things that can go wrong during delivery.

Cliff: The first three months after Tim was born were the hardest three months I've ever experienced. Part of the difficulty was learning to sleep only four or five hours a night. When I came home from work at night I took over the care of our son so my wife could get some rest. Whenever he cried in the night, I was the one who got up and tried to get him back to sleep. He had colic so I was up about five times a night. It was the hardest thing I've ever done.

Mike: I already had two boys (I have legally adopted my wife's two sons), so Lisa was our first biological child. I was wondering what my feelings would be. We took the Lamaze classes and were together during the whole birth process. It was the highest ecstacy—wonder—jubilation. We were all higher than a kite. And of course we were very excited to have a girl. It sort of completed our family, but it made our house smaller! I hadn't experienced the boys' birth so I learned what it meant to be up late at night, walking the baby, and that sort of thing. It was a vicarious experiencing of the boys' birth and early infancy.

How involved were you with caring for the physical needs of your first child?

Paul: In the beginning, not very much. But after James was about six months old, with the pressure and needs for two incomes, Sue began to work part-time. I found myself much more involved. I was a little uncomfortable in the beginning, but I came around. I was fighting that role. I didn't *want* to change diapers. That diaper stage is a hard one. I have trouble with that. It's not a very pleasant thing.

Glenn: The first 10 days of Tracy's life I'm the one who changed her diapers, because Annette had had a hard time in delivery and was in bed. With our second daughter, I was house-husband for about four months before her birth. My wife was flat on her back with the doctors telling us there was no way the baby could live. It gave me a real appreciation for the woman who has to maintain the dual roles of trying to hold the household together and also earn a living. Between the crock pot and the microwave my life was saved!

Generally, Annette takes care of the children during the night because I have to work the next day. But from about 5:00 A.M. on I'm in charge because she doesn't get up early easily. There is such a short time that we can have that kind of a relationship with a child. Even when the diapers and all are a bit of a pain, those are really cherished moments.

Cliff: I did everything except nursing! Before we had Tim I used to watch the way my friends took care of their little daughter. I could never imagine myself doing some of the things they did— like cutting up the meat on her plate first while their own got cold. When Tim came along, doing those things seemed like second nature. That was a pleasant surprise. I didn't expect it.

Mike: When Lynae and I knew we were getting married I would often bathe the boys and get them ready for bed, and I would change Joshua who was barely two years old. The first time he told me he loved me was when I was getting him ready for bed and changing his diaper. Since our marriage I'm quite actively involved in sharing the roles. Sometimes if Lynae was with Lisa, I would take care of the boys and fix dinner. If she needed sleep, I'd look after Lisa.

Glenn: I think one advantage to being older when I married and had a child is that I could learn from other people's experiences. I have talked to a lot of people who had children, including fathers who didn't spend much time with their children during the early years and later really regretted it. My perspective is that even though a lot of caring for a child is a hassle, it's an opportunity I won't have again.

What was the biggest adjustment you had to make when your first child was born?

Mike: Probably time and freedom. I became more of a servant to the children. My free time came when they were at school or with a baby-sitter. Or early morning or late at night. I have had to become more creative about some of my projects in order to get them accomplished. I also find it hard to be consistent when I am exhausted. The children run out the door to greet me when I come home, which is great. But sometimes I'm really tired and I need just a little space. Parenting takes lots of energy.

Paul: I had a real struggle with my time commitments. I had a strong desire to work with high school and college kids and I was involved with them at church. All through high school and college I was used to every night out. But it finally came down to whether I was going to put my life into high school kids, or into my own kid. It was tough going, but the right decision was that I needed to spend more time at home.

Cliff: Before children I was in control of my life, but now I'm not. There are so many things that I know I should be taking responsibility for, but I just never get around to them.

Glenn: In many respects the second child coming along was more of an adjustment than the first. Before that, when I would travel for two- or three-day trips, Annette and Tracy would always go with me. When Melissa came along, a woman with two very small children in a hotel room does not work out very well.

Mike: When the first child arrives, husband and wife are no longer the only person in each other's lives. And with each succeeding child there is one more person with whom we share our affection. I have known families for whom that would be a problem. For us it is no problem, largely because of Lynae's clearly-stated feelings to me that "we love our children, but they are not you and they do not take the place of you." And I feel the same toward her. The kids are aware of that, too. There are some times when we say, "Go in the other room, we need some time together."

In what area do you feel most confident as a father?

Glenn: You can spoil a child with things. You can't spoil him with love. Annette and I both love our children very much. There may be some rough edges in our parenting, but I think the children will turn out basically alright just because we are doing it with the right attitude.

Mike: I'm confident of my commitments to my children and of my ability to express my affection for them. My boys love to wrestle. Their favorite thing is to wrestle with Dad. I'm confident that the modeling I'm doing is good. They all want to learn to be cooks!

Paul: Babies are not a comfortable age for me. But now that James is four I really enjoy him. We have a lot of fun together. It's fun to talk to him because he's old enough now to carry on an intelligent conversation. I get a response that I didn't get when he was a baby. I was so impressed when he was finally old enough to give me a hug or a kiss. That's such a warm thing from a child. A baby can't do that. When your child comes up to you out of the blue and says, "I like you," or gives you a hug, that's really a neat thing.

Cliff: I feel confident about my ability to relate to my children in different ways and circumstances because of how much I practice it.

In what area do you feel most inadequate as a father?

Mike: I feel inadequate in my ability to be always "on." Sometimes when I'm tired I get irritable. I'm confident that my children love me and forgive me. But I can't abuse that relationship. I want my children to value a relationship with me when they are grown up. That's why I'm trying to build a relationship with them now.

Glenn: The primary inadequacy I feel is in achieving a balance between controlling a child's behavior so that you help him learn to deal with society, and allowing him enough freedom to be an individual. I don't want my children to become submissive robots, but neither do I want to raise little brats who won't be accepted by their peers. I have worked with a lot of delinquents and have heard strapping football players crying and saying, "I wish my dad loved me enough to hit me." Or girls saying, "I wish my mom loved me enough to slap me when I get out of line." They relate discipline with love. I wrestle with this and Annette and I talk about it. I guess I won't know until sometime after the fact whether we've struck a balance.

Cliff: I feel inadequate in the area of fulfilling the role of head of the household. It's actually the relationship with my wife that makes me feel inadequate as a father. It comes out in two areas: (1) I don't think we're giving our children a biblical model of what a father and mother/husband and wife are supposed to be, at least not close enough to my satisfaction; (2) The other area is the "family altar"—praying together, studying the Bible together, communicating feelings such as resentment toward one another and getting things ironed out. I believe in those things, but we don't do them because I am not a good leader and my wife is not a good follower. By personality, she is the leader and I am the follower.

Paul: Sometimes it's hard to want to relate to James. When I get home at night I'm tired. In the morning I get him dressed, fix his breakfast and take him to nursery school. In the pressure to get him to school and me to work on time, it's hard to want to relate to him in the car. I'm trying to pursue a career, live out my faith, and bring up my son. There's a lot of pressure there because I want to achieve in all those areas. Every day I have to make choices. Life was so much simpler when I was 10!

How has parenthood changed your relationship with your wife?

Cliff: Children have improved our relationship because it's something we do as a team. Before the kids there was very little we did together that was real teamwork. One of the surprises of the birth experience was how well we worked together using the Lamaze method. My coaching was good, she responded to it and it helped her. That was really the first time I realized she needed me and appreciated my help. And we have continued to work as a team with the children because we are both needed.

Mike: My whole process of wooing Lynae was also in terms of almost dating her boys. By the time we were married I was well into the life of the boys and functioning in the father role. I must say, however, that when we came back from our honeymoon, the greatest shock was waking up that first morning with my new wife and suddenly hearing, "Daddy! Daddy!" at seven in the morning. The honeymoon was over and I had two boys, just like that!

Paul: There was some stress in terms of who's going to take care of which responsibilities—what was fair and equitable. And there was less time to ourselves. I think the idea that "it isn't how much time you spend together, it's *quality* time that counts" is a lot of baloney. There may be some truth to that, but I haven't found it to be so. I think you have to spend *more* time together as husband and wife.

What do you most appreciate about your wife as a mother?

Glenn: Our society doesn't put a whole lot of value on the role of the mother. I am frustrated by that, but I have a great respect for the way my wife is able to fulfill that role, despite not having a lot of strokes from society. Annette is a very bright, accomplished person in her own right. I appreciate so much the fact that she can devote herself fully to mothering, while people around her are chiding that "she's just a housewife." Especially when she has the ability to go out and do more than many of the women who are bragging that they have broken out of the "prison" of the home and are pursuing other interests. I find it absolutely amazing that a woman will destroy her marriage in pursuit of a career and end up being a secretary somewhere. Seeing how Annette has responded to her new role has brought me closer to her.

Cliff: I respect my wife more because I see her put a lot into mothering and I discover she's good at it. It's a facet of her I couldn't know before we had children. In addition to having to defend her role to society, I find my wife sometimes defends *me* to her more "liberated" friends when they hear me being what they think is too supportive of her role as a mother. It's a strange position for a woman to be in.

Paul: I appreciate the fact that most of the time my wife knows all the right things to do for our son. At other times, I appreciate the fact that we can share the same frustrations of *not* knowing what to do. Like when the baby cries in the middle of the night and neither of us knows what to do. I appreciate her for her competence but also for, at times, our shared incompetence.

Mike: I appreciate the fact that my wife fosters the romance of our relationship. And she does not do it at the expense of her care for the children. She has a clear understanding of the priority of our relationship. She does not live for her children, yet she loves her children. We treasure the long-term relationship that we will have after the children are gone.

Another thing I appreciate is that she has interests, dreams, desires and ambitions that I also value, and that makes her more attractive to me. That's exciting to me. That turns me on.

What do you least understand about your wife as a mother?

Glenn: Chemical changes take place during the month that make my wife act differently. We talk about it and joke about it. But because I haven't gone through it I really can't understand it.

Paul: I don't really understand those emotional changes either. Neither can I identify with the physical aspects of pregnancy—backaches, something kicking inside her stomach. My wife knows when the baby is asleep and when it is awake. I can't understand that because I've never experienced it.

Mike: I have difficulty comprehending my wife's ability to care on so many fronts. The constancy of her care at so many different levels within the family is a very demanding thing. Sometimes I just don't know where she gets her energy. For example, this past week she's been having some frustration because when she is in the bathroom in the morning getting ready for the day, we usually all end up in there with her. I attribute that to our desire to be with her. And there are also various demands: "Mommy, I need this." "Mom, will you check my homework?" Lisa wants to be held. And I want to visit with her. Sometimes it's important for us to give her space.

What one thing do you most want your wife to understand about your role as a father?

Glenn: I most want my wife to understand how seriously I take my role as a father. I continually struggle with the balance between how much time to spend on income generation versus time spent with the family. Being a father is my most important job. Part of my reason for being so serious about my role is that I have seen so many men who weren't, until it was too late.

Cliff: I think one of the primary hurdles in a father becoming more involved with his children is knowing enough about it to be confident. A woman has a strong desire to prove herself a worthy mother. The wife needs to be aware that her husband is probably feeling even more inse-cure than she is. He could use some encourage-ment and affirmation in his role as a father.

Glenn: Affirmation as opposed to badgering. I've heard mothers say to their husbands, "*Your son* needs changing." I think she does this partly to show her friends that, yes, she's got this turkey help-ing her. Rather than encouraging him, she's really nagging. If he is not comfortable with fathering, she is actually insulting him by her attitude.

Cliff: Also, her attitude may not be a true reflection of just how involved the father really is. When I am at home I am actually more involved with my children than my wife is. (She cares for them when I am at work.) If she were to imply in public that she has to tell me to help out and how to do it, that would hurt.

Glenn: I think a lot of dads deep down would like to be more involved with their children, but they don't know how. In the "macho" cultures where the roles are rigidly defined, the man is off playing cards while the woman is at home with the children. A close friend who is from a "macho" culture has commented several times, "I wish I were as comfortable with children as you are." He doesn't really know how to relate to his children, but he's working on it. Since there is very little push toward fathering in our society, most fathers don't get any support in trying to follow their instincts.

Mike: My wife understands pretty well the pressure of the ministry that is constantly before me and my struggles to succeed in my work. It's an ongoing tension. An area we are working on right now is finding time for each of us to be alone. By the time we get the children in bed it's easily nine o'clock and we are both just beat. So the only time we end up with is late at night and then we're tired in the morning. I'm having to become an early-morning person in order to achieve that alone time.

What are your spiritual goals for your family and how are you attempting to achieve them?

Paul: Our basic desire is that James know who Jesus Christ is and who God is and that he establish a relationship with God that he is comfortable with. We want him to feel good about our Christian life together, that it's a natural thing to do, not artificial. The three of us ate at a restaurant tonight and James brought his Bible storybook with him. He would look at the picture of Jesus dying on the cross and ask us to read the story to him. One or the other of us prays with him at night. If there is a problem and all three of us are involved in it, we all three pray together about it. When he laughs or starts playing around when we are praying, we always try to bring that into line. Talking to God is serious business. We're not playing games.

Cliff: I believe that for kids to come through the teen years with the least amount of stress and the greatest possibility of retaining the Christian faith, they have to have seen it in action. It's not a religion we do. It's a natural part of us, because God is real. A healthy respect for the possibility of the kids rejecting Christ is a good deal of what drives me to invest so much now. I am convinced that by the time children are five years of age their personalities and attitudes are pretty well set. I'm afraid that if I don't lay a good foundation for them now, when they are teenagers I won't be able to remedy the situation. Without a good foundation, the house might fall down.

Glenn: I'm concerned about the physical welfare of my children, but their eternal salvation is much more important. I agree with Cliff that the early years are very, very critical. When my oldest daughter was four she asked Jesus to come into her heart. I don't know if she comprehended fully what she was doing, but she still talks about it. Before the children were born, we were not in the habit of saying grace before meals. Now, saying grace and also prayers at bedtime are a natural part of our lives. It is also important to us to start our children's schooling in a Christian school.

Mike: I have several goals for my children. One is modeling for them—a congruence of emotional expressions and verbalized spiritual commitments. That means that when I'm tired, for instance, I still have to be mature in Christ.

In the past I have spent an hour a week alone with each of our boys. Christopher and I would go jogging and maybe work on learning a verse of Scripture. I keep a record in my journal of significant interactions with him so that I can maintain a history of my relationship with him. More and more I am taking him with me to ministry functions. Yesterday I had to go to a convalescent home with some collegians and I took both boys with me. Christopher read Scripture and Joshua sang "Jesus Loves Me" (he's not at all intimidated by adults). Including them like that lets them share in my ministry and also develop ministries of their own.

With Joshua (who's five) I try to spend a significant amount of time playing with him. My wife was with both of the boys when they asked Jesus into their hearts.

My other goal is that they would treasure my counsel. But I have to earn that right. There is a song about a father/son relationship. When the son is small the father is too busy for the son. It comes to a point where the father is now ready for a relationship, but the son is too busy for the father. The father always wanted the son to be like him. The paradox is: He is.

A Resource: For quick and profitable reading I highly recommend a monthly newsletter titled *For Dads Only*. Each issue contains items such as: short tips on how to relate to your children; activities to do together; an article about an effective father; a brief article on a subject of interest to fathers; and reviews of various resources. For further information write to Paul Lewis, Editor, *For Dads Only*, P.O. Box 20594, San Diego, California 92120.

Note
1. Maxine Hancock, *People in Progress* (Old Tappan, NJ: Fleming H. Revell Co., 1978), p. 19. Used by permission of Maxine Hancock.

CHAPTER 3

No carbon copies

I used to have great respect for the capabilities of Houdini. But when our boys began to crawl and climb, I concluded that Houdini did nothing any boy can't do. Our boys could get into, under, over and out of absolutely anything. If Houdini had been a woman, I decided, he never would have made it as a magician.

But I was wrong about Houdini—and about boys. Because not all boys are like ours. Chad, my friend's two-year-old boy, is calm and docile. When I have had him in my home at nap time, I lay him down on the bed and cover him up. He doesn't seem to move until I peek in sometime later to see if he is awake. My sons would have been up on the chandelier.

The differences in children are dramatic.

One of the joys of parenting is discovering the total uniqueness of each and every child. Just when you think you've got parenting down pat, along comes child number two or three or four.

Child number one is calm and easygoing, responds well to discipline, and entertains himself most of the day. Aren't all children like that?

Then along comes number two. A sensitive, intense child, he

hears every noise and notices every movement. The first child eats anything and everything. The second child has definite likes and dislikes and often picks at his food. You realize with the suddenness of a thunderbolt that with children there are no duplicates. After every child, God throws away the mold. That's one of the most precious revelations of parenthood.

For the first few years of her life, our daughter was shy and fearful in new situations. She frequently clung to me and needed my reassurance and my presence.

Then along came the boys. As shy and retiring as Shana was, they were the opposite. They are friendly and outgoing, ready to make friends with the whole world. I delight in watching the two types of personalities at work. Shana's caution is necessary in many situations. The boys' enthusiasm for making friends is necessary in others. Neither approach is wrong. They are simply different ways of approaching life.

Reed is willing to try new foods. Sardines are on his okay list. So are artichokes. Scott likes to spend time alone building things or playing with a toy. Shana has developed an interest in the piano. Each has certain capabilities and limitations. As their interests change and develop, their life's focus will begin to come into view. What a fascinating process to watch!

A feeling of deep appreciation for your children's uniqueness is one of the by-products of parenting. With your first child you were probably a little uptight with certain expectations at the forefront of your mind. With subsequent children you feel more relaxed. I believe the first child will always be the family "guinea pig" as we test our parenting skills and seek ways to relate. We feel apprehensive about number one because the first child's experiences are new to us.

Some parents miss the appreciation of their children's uniqueness because they have preconceived notions of what children ought to be like. In particular, of what *their* children ought to be like.

In one family scholastic ability may be the goal. In another it may be athletics. Some fathers expect their sons to carry on the family business. Other parents expect their children to achieve success in areas in which they never were able to achieve themselves. Like the aspiring actress whose career is cut short by motherhood. In an effort to experience vicariously the fame she missed, she pushes her daughter onto the stage. Or the father who always wanted to be a big-time ball player. His son had better pursue athletics, or else.

"My ex-husband was big on athletics," a woman told me the other day. "When my son was nine he pushed him into Little League. I remember a ball game where my son was up there swinging his bat for all he was worth. But because he didn't make a home run his father really got on him. I was so mad at him! What's so important about a home run?"

One of the saddest cases I know of is a mother who appears never to have accepted the fact that her son is not the daughter she wanted.

I think it does all of us good once in a while to ask ourselves just exactly *why* we have brought our children into this world. Was it so your child would—
— Carry on the family name?
— Give the world a great scientist, author, athlete or businessman?
— Achieve what you could not?
— Be molded into your own image and likeness?
— Become a loving human being who loves God and serves his fellow man?

A child owes his parents nothing—except respect. *You* owe *him* a great deal, because by your choice—not his—he came into the world helpless, defenseless, in need of protection and care. When he is grown and gone, he does not owe you anything for all the years of your labor. Nothing, that is, except respect. He does not owe you vicarious fame, or back pats from your friends over the terrific kid you've raised. You, however, owe him everything. And one of the most important things you owe him is your acceptance of him, just the way he is.

Does this mean that you accept his early attributes as set in concrete? Certainly not. Along with our individual characteristics comes lots of immaturity and the sin nature with which we all are born. A rude child needs to be corrected. A shy child needs to be exposed to other children and adults. An only child needs to spend time with other children so he will learn to share.

Sometimes you will be attracted to one child's personality more than to another. Some children are easier to get along with than others. But it does not change your love and acceptance of your other children. By no means should such feelings be construed as playing favorites.

At the heart of your acceptance is a deep-seated appreciation for the worth of another human being, a belief in the right of each child to become his own person, and a commitment to demonstrate to that child how important it is to you that he be his own unique self.

"Nurturing love," says Dorothy Briggs in *Your Child's Self-Esteem*, "is tender caring—valuing a child just because he exists. It comes when you see your youngster as special and dear—*even though you may not approve of all that he does.*"[1]

My parents have always believed I could do anything I really wanted to. I will appreciate their confidence in me to my dying day. It's a legacy I want to pass on to my children.

One of the dangers in not appreciating our children's individual differences is that we may end up comparing them with children whose behavior is more acceptable to us. Behavior that better fits the "image" of what we want our child to be.

Families tend to take on a personality all their own. If a particular child fits into that personality, he or she is made to feel a member. If the individual doesn't he or she is often marked as "the different one." Parents and other siblings sometimes use humor to set the child aside and make him or her feel unworthy. Sometimes, sadly, they use ridicule and even abuse.[2]

Parents of young children should make it a point to let the children know they are acceptable in spite of (not because of) their size, their features, their running speed, and their motivation. If a husky, well-coordinated boy would rather write stories than play softball, that should be his right. And he shouldn't have to overhear his parents apologizing for him, either. Likewise, parents must be careful to avoid the obvious valuing of a child who *does* show physical prowess or who is large. Children often take parents' praise for other children as a rebuke for their lack of stature or interest.[3]

I was reading recently about a 16-year-old girl who had developed anorexia nervosa—weight loss and severe malnutrition caused by a hysterical aversion to food. In the course of her recovery, her entire family became involved in therapy. During the therapy her mother discovered the excessive demands she had placed on her daughter. The daughter explains:

> Since she had pigeonholed my older sister as the pretty, nervous child, and my younger sister as the artistic one, she could allow them their temper tantrums and moods. But because I was her "well-adjusted" daughter, she made me feel that any rebelliousness on my part would be out of character and unacceptable. My mother was stunned by my illness, but her counseling sessions helped her understand how her attitude had influenced the emotional lives of her children.[4]

Accepting your child's uniqueness is something you do from the moment he is born. And you do it all your life.

One of the things that has helped me understand and appreciate my children's differences has been Dr. James Dobson's book, *The Strong-Willed Child.* Until I read his views, I thought that quiet, well-behaved children were the result of their parents' marvelous upbringing. Aggressive, defiant children were the result of permissive parents who let their kids get away with murder. Dr. Dobson says "that ain't necessarily so."

From the time she was old enough to respond to discipline, Shana has been easy to handle. Simply a cross look could dissolve her into tears and bring about the desired change.

Then along came my sons. Instead of dissolving into tears over a spanking (a cross look meant nothing), the strong-willed one would look me in the eye instead and say defiantly, "That didn't hurt" and refuse to shed a tear. If I told Shana to stop doing something, she quit. If I told my son, he might immediately seek ways to do it without getting caught. *What am I doing wrong?* I thought, in bewilderment. Then I began reading *The*

Strong-Willed Child. And I learned that Shana is a compliant child. She thrives on the rewards she receives for being good.

> The easygoing child is often a genuine charmer. He smiles at least sixteen hours a day and spends most of his time trying to figure out what his parents want and how he can make them happy. In reality, he *needs* their praise and approval; thus his personality is greatly influenced by this desire to gain their affection and recognition.[5]

I could identify with that description. I was that kind of a child.

I also learned that my more defiant son is that way, not because I'm doing something wrong as a parent, but because that's the personality he was born with. Dr. Dobson explains:

> Just as surely as some children are naturally compliant, there are others who seem to be defiant upon exit from the womb. They come into the world smoking a cigar and yelling about the temperature in the delivery room and the incompetence of the nursing staff and the way things are run by the administrator of the hospital. They expect meals to be served the instant they are ordered, and they demand every moment of mother's time. As the months unfold, their expression of willfulness becomes even more apparent, the winds reaching hurricane force during toddlerhood.[6]

While shaping the will of a defiant child is much more difficult and requires great wisdom on the part of the parents, the picture is by no means all negative. Strong-willed children have great potential for developing a strong character and leading a productive life. "However, the realization of that potential," warns Dr. Dobson, "may depend on a firm but loving early home environment."[7]

Not all children fall precisely into these two categories, however. There are plenty of children who lie somewhere in between. The value of understanding these two types is: (a) you are relieved of the guilt of thinking that the defiant child is the product of your own making, nor can you take all the credit for the behavior of your compliant child; and (b) it should make you more tolerant of your friends whose children are opposite from yours. Your children and theirs are what they are because that's the way God made them. Each child must be helped to grow and develop within the bounds of his own personality. I highly recommend Dr. Dobson's book for his discussion on how to shape a child's will without breaking it.

One of the ways we help children discover their interests and abilities is by exposing them to many different experiences.

Shana started piano instruction a few months ago. When her childish "banging" changed to "playing" (albeit without a melody), I realized that she was ready for lessons. At the moment she's making progress and enjoying her learning experience. A year from now she may no longer be interested in the piano. If her disinterest continues, we will stop the lessons. But at least she will have had a chance.

Visiting museums and historic places, taking art or music lessons, learning various sports exposes a child to many things which some day he may decide to pursue in earnest. Not that a child should be involved in too many activities. But it is important, I feel, for a child to learn to do at least one thing well.

When I was a teenager I was very shy. I never ran with the "popular" crowd; I had many dateless nights. I was what you call a "late bloomer."

My teen years were riddled with self-doubt, insecurities, a real inferiority complex. But in one area I shone. I could play the piano and most of my friends could not. At church I was in demand to play for Sunday School, church, youth meetings, what have you. And I sometimes played at school as well. At church I was "somebody" and it got me through those difficult years. I shall always be grateful that my parents helped me find one thing I was good at and encouraged me to pursue it.

Within the compliant-defiant spectrum there are a whole host of different personality types. Numerous books have been written describing why one person is one way and another is so different.

My husband and I are two quite different personalities in many ways. He is a night person. I am a day person. At 8:00 in the morning he has trouble bringing the world into focus. I'm up and ready to go. But he can work until 2:00 or 3:00 the next morning without the slightest difficulty. By 10:00 or 11:00 at night, *my* world has lost its focus.

I am a goal-oriented person. I like to know where I'm going in life and how long it's going to take me to get there. I'm not satisfied unless I'm trying to accomplish something. I operate on a time schedule. The clock and I are close friends.

My husband's approach is quite different. He sets and achieves goals, but in a much different manner than I. I am the family time clock. He is the one who helps us take time to smell the flowers.

Sometimes, like any couple, we get on each other's nerves. He gets tired of my tendency to want to schedule his time. I am not always understanding of his need to relax after a hectic day or week at work. But when we allow our personalities to complement each other, we can appreciate each other for what we are.

How dreadful if both of us were clock watchers. Or if neither of us cared what time we got up or went to bed. The differences in our personalities help us both to grow and mature. Sometimes when my husband does something that irritates me, or vice versa, we remind ourselves that that is one of the characteristics of our mate's personality type. And since we really *like* each other's personality, a petty annoyance is prevented from becoming a full-blown war.

Just so, there will be things we both like and dislike about our children's personalities. And, since maturity is a life-time goal, there will be areas where they genuinely need to change. Those changes will come more easily, I think, if our children are assured of the fact that no matter what they do or don't do, our love for them never, ever changes.

The rewards of such an attitude are many. By accepting our children just as God made them, we are free to sit back and watch the unfolding of a beautiful, brand new life. What our children *do* in life becomes much less important than what they *are*. Instead of trying to make them become something they were never intended to be, we free them to become all God wants them to be. As we ask God for the wisdom that only He can give, He will help us guide our little ones to the pinnacle of their capacities. (We must remember, of course, that each child has his own will. He is *free not* to choose what is right as surely as he is free to choose what *is*.) In essence, we become partners with God in the exciting adventure of helping His children become complete.

Through the conformance of our wills to God's will, we become partakers of the miraculous.

Notes
1. Dorothy Corkille Briggs, *Your Child's Self-Esteem* (Garden City, NY: Doubleday and Company, Inc., 1975), pp. 61,62.
2. Dolores Curran, "God Always Breaks the Mold," *Christian Parenting: The Young Child* (New York: Paulist Press, 1979), p. 30. Used by permission of the Missionary Society of St. Paul the Apostle in the state of New York.
3. Ibid., p. 32.
4. Anna Cramer, "The Starvation of Anna," *Family Circle Magazine*, August 26, 1980, p. 15. Used by permission of Jamie Raab.
5. James Dobson, *The Strong-Willed Child* (Wheaton, IL: Tyndale House Publishers, 1978), p. 23.
6. Ibid., p. 20.
7. Ibid., p. 25.

CHAPTER 4

When will I sleep
through the night?

Jill's son was four when the twins were born. A few weeks later I invited her to go to a Mothers of Twins Club meeting with me. The babies were not yet sleeping through the night and she hadn't had enough sleep to write home about. She called the night of the meeting and our conversation went something like this:

"I'm planning to go," she said, "at least I hope I can go. I haven't been feeling very well. To tell you the truth, I've been having these bad headaches. And sometimes I feel like I'm going to pass out."

"You haven't had much sleep, have you?" I asked, knowing the intensity of sleeplessness that only a mother of twins (triplets, quadruplets) can experience.

"Not much," she continued, not yet getting the point of my question. "I went to the doctor because I was afraid maybe I have a brain tumor but he checked me and said there's nothing wrong."

"There's nothing wrong with you that a good night's sleep won't cure," I said.

"He said the only other thing to do would be to take x-rays

and run some tests," she continued. "I don't know whether to go ahead with it or not, but I am concerned there might be a tumor." Fatigue was playing tricks with her mind.

"All you need is a good night's sleep." I tried again, remembering my own sons' first weeks when the days and nights seemed to run together.

"I'll try and come to the meeting tonight. But if I should start to pass out, will you take me home?" she asked.

"Of course, but you'll really be okay after some sleep."

Her husband came on the phone to get directions to the meeting place. Hoping that *his* brain had not been dulled by lack of sleep, I repeated what I had been telling her. "There's nothing wrong with your wife," I said, "that a couple of good nights of sleep won't cure."

And in subsequent weeks (and with some hired help for the nighttime feedings) she discovered for herself that there was in fact no brain tumor at all. She was simply exhausted.

The first year with our boys was a marathon of work. Friends who came to visit followed me from room to room if they wanted to talk. If I stopped working I would get behind. Even with help—and compared with some mothers I had quite a bit—it was like being on a treadmill. How many times, perhaps only my husband knows for sure, he would come home from work and find me sitting alone (if at all possible) on the front porch. On the really frantic days I might be pacing up and down in the front yard with one or two babies in my arms waiting for him to come home.

"I'm not going back in there," I would say, pointing to the house. "It's all yours."

ACCUMULATED FATIGUE

"I believe fatigue to be the greatest enemy a woman ever faces," wrote the late Dr. Marion Hilliard, chief of Obstetrics and Gynecology at Women's College Hospital in Toronto, in her book *Women and Fatigue*. She continues:

> Fatigue is something you can enjoy and not be afraid of. The normal fatigue that follows accomplishment—regardless of whether the process has been

pleasant or unpleasant—*should* be enjoyed. Rest, relax, and you will be revived by one good night's sleep.

It's the fatigue you have accumulated, the fatigue that's too great to be dispersed by normal rest or a night or two of good sleep, that can spell trouble for you.

This kind of fatigue can happen to the woman who has filled her social or business schedule too full, just as it can to the woman who is nursing an invalid or caring for a family of small children. . . . The woman who "does too much," even though she loves every minute of it, is wearing out her adrenal glands. Maybe not as fast as she would with too many unpleasant chores, but she is still heading for fatigue.[1]

In its chronic stage fatigue is characterized over a period of months or years by dullness, apathy, and a general disinterest in life. It is often accompanied by physical symptoms such as headaches, backaches, depression, crying spells.

"To the chronically fatigued person, nothing seems very important," says Dr. John L. Bulette, psychiatrist and the director of general-hospital psychiatry at the Medical College of Pennsylvania.[2]

On the other end of the spectrum is the fatigue suffered daily by mothers of small children. The kind of fatigue that means you are tired and exhausted from the events of the day, but after a good night's sleep you're ready to start over.

For some reason women seem to be more prone to fatigue than men. Dr. Hilliard suggests three periods in a woman's life when she is particularly susceptible to fatigue: adolescence, pregnancy, and menopause. Each of these periods of fatigue is caused by the chemical changes taking place in her body. The first few months after the birth of a child can be a time of enormous fatigue. Our body chemistry is changing back to the pre-pregnancy days. And our children have not yet learned that nighttime is for sleep.

Recognizing these periods frees us to make sure we get adequate rest and relaxation. Some of us have high energy levels, some lower. By carefully studying our particular high/low pattern we can determine just how much rest we need to stay healthy and serene. And nothing but rest will do it.

In his book, *The Stress of Life,* Dr. Hans Selye, a leading authority on stress, contends that there are three stages through which a person passes in his reaction to stress. The first stage is the "alarm" stage when the body (particularly the endocrine glands and the nervous system) sends out messages that something stressful has happened—a severe burn, a cut, an illness, a broken romance. In the second stage, called the "stage of resistance," the body begins to adapt. You learn to live with the pain, the illness, or the fact of a lost love. If the stress is too stressful and lasts too long, however, the third stage goes into effect—the "stage of exhaustion." He calls this process the general adaptation syndrome (G.A.S.).

During the "stage of resistance" the body adapts to stress in various ways, depending on certain physical factors (such as heredity) and emotional factors (how well we know ourselves). Applied to mothers of young children, the adaptation process can easily include physical symptoms such as headaches, backaches, or beating your frustrations out on a pillow. If resentments and other negative emotions are smoldering under the surface, our adaptation may have similar manifestations, but for different reasons. The mother who screams a little now and then or beats a sofa pillow to a pulp has a lot better chance for survival than the mother who lets stressful situations turn into bitterness and resentment. For the one the stress is but for a moment. For the other it may be for a lifetime.

Two things are important for mothers of preschoolers: (1) you must learn to deal with daily stress constructively lest it build until you become chronically fatigued, and (2) you need not feel guilty because you are too tired to move at the end of the day. It's part of being a mother of young children. Only mothers with full-time nannies can escape it!

What is it about small children that makes being around them so fulfilling—and yet so exhausting?

Have you ever worked with or been around an adult who was very immature? Chances are the person talked a lot about himself, talked a lot period! Argued. Pouted or cried when he didn't get his way. Frequently interrupted you. Had little sense of responsibility. "Didn't know when to come in out of the rain," as the saying goes.

How did you feel at the end of the day after being around him for a long period of time? Probably exhausted. The smooth flow of conversation and work that generally flows between two adults just wasn't there. You continually had to be on your guard. You never knew what to expect next.

By comparison I have just described a day with preschoolers. The difference, however, is that there are few rewarding moments with an immature adult because he's not likely to see the error of his ways or seek to change. With children, the rewards are many, even though they are often spaced a long way apart. In between are the pouting, crying, arguing, and interrupting, and the constant teaching you must do to change them from immature, irresponsible little savages into the well-behaved, adorable little children you always knew they could be.

If you are exhausted at the end of the day, you have a right to be. You worked for it. Just knowing you are responsible for the *physical* safety of your active toddlers is awesome. Even when you make every attempt to baby-proof your house, children who are "climbers" can still find heights and depths you never dreamed possible. (How well I remember visiting with a friend when it suddenly occurred to me that the house was too quiet. Where were my two toddler boys? We went searching. The first thing we found was the chandelier over the eating table swinging back and forth—but nary a boy in sight.)

Toddlers can be exhausting. What can you do to combat fatigue? Quite frankly, I can't offer a solution that will eliminate it. It's part of the preschool-parenting package. Like other things mentioned in the last chapter of this book, "it, too, will pass."

Once the children are all in school, mothers generally feel as frisky as colts. They spend hours wandering through department stores, attending fashion shows, bazaars . . . luncheons. . . . Late in the afternoon they hurtle home, slam some pots and pans on the stove, deal with an avalanche of leggy youngsters and end up with as big a case of fatigue as when the children were small. A woman continually must arrange her life to give herself time to relax. If her children are in school then she must realize that her work period is concentrated at the end of the day; somewhere in the early afternoon she has to find time to rest with her feet up.[3]

Dr. Hilliard describes a typical fatigue case: a woman in her twenties in good physical condition with two children under school age. She is complaining of a headache or backache.

"Of course your back aches," I tell her briskly; sympathy is not going to be particularly helpful. "You have two preschool children and you're tired out. You can expect to be tired, all the time, until they are in school."

I have given up looking for a solution for this problem: There isn't one. A woman who has a baby has to face up to the realization that she will be tired for the next five years. The preschool child needs constant attention twenty-four hours a day for five years. She must supervise his meals, train him to go to the bathroom, dress himself, protect himself from automobiles and rainstorms, teach him the English language and social deportment, nurse him when he is sick, and comfort him through his nightmares. Certainly she is tired.[4]

There are, however, some things you can do to reduce the amount of fatigue you experience and, most importantly, to keep it from reaching the chronic stage.

FIGHTING FATIGUE

Get as much rest as possible. "It's *not* possible," you say, especially if your child is not yet sleeping through the night. It *is* possible, but to do it you must adapt your schedule to the child's. That means sleeping or resting when *he* is napping, be it day or night. Broken sleep is never as good as uninterrupted sleep, but it's better than no sleep at all. The dishes will wait. The diapers can be folded later (or maybe you should buy prefolded ones and use them right out of the laundry basket). Your husband can survive one more night of leftovers, especially if they are served by a cheerful wife instead of a grouch.

One of my favorite games when my three were still taking naps was to get them all bedded down (and asleep) at the same time. Within minutes I was on the couch. The game, I admit, required as much chance as it did skill. But when it occurred I took immediate advantage of the situation and slept. It's the only way I would have made it through dinner.

Change your surroundings. It is an enormous job to get a small child (or two, or three, or four, or more) ready for an outing. By the time you have changed and rechanged them, packed enough diapers, bottles, and changes of clothes, you wonder if a trip to the park or a friend's house is really worth the effort. Believe me, it is! Physically, it may be just as much work as staying home. But mentally it will give you a new lift. A change of scenery never hurt anybody, especially when you are all beginning to get on each other's nerves.

Vary your routine. My husband was working late one night and I was extremely tired. I dreaded the hassle of baths, hustling the children into p.j.s while they preferred to dawdle, and the "yes, we can have just one more story tonight" bit. So I decided to vary the routine.

"You may each wear each other's pajamas to bed," I told the children. "Shana can wear Scott's, Scott can wear Reed's, and Reed can wear Shana's."

They were delighted and scurried off to find what they would wear and what they would give each other to wear. Scott's Superman pajamas were too little for Shana so she wore another pair that were roomier. Scott was delighted with Reed's "jogging jamas." I'm not sure what the child psychologists would say about Reed running around in his sister's ruffled nightgown.

The next thing I knew they swapped beds as well. Everyone was happy and bedtime was much less of a drain on Mom.

Experiments have a way of taking unexpected twists, however. In the middle of the night Reed decided to come into our bed.

"I have to go potty first," he informed me (that's the rule, to prevent bed-wetting). "But how can I?" he asked, standing in the doorway in ruffled splendor.

I thought he needed some light. So I told him he could use either bathroom, knowing that the one in his room has a night light.

"But how can I?" he kept asking. Finally it dawned on me. A little boy of three has no idea what to do with a *nightgown* when he has to go potty!

"That's one problem you never have to deal with," I muttered into the darkness as I held up all that yardage so he could appease Mother Nature.

Avoid becoming over-involved. After 35 years of rushing about and being involved in everything, having children has taught me the importance of not programming myself so tightly. I still have a few involvements in church and elsewhere. But I learned early in the game that when I took on too many activities I would soon become frantic because I could not meet my obligations. The casserole has to be ready in an hour for the potluck we don't really need to attend, and my toddler hasn't given me a moment to even look for the recipe. The magazine article is due next Wednesday and I haven't had time to work on it since last week.

And do you know what a frantic mother does? She yells at her children (at least this one does). I finally concluded that, for the most part, participation in anything that has a deadline (e.g., meeting time, due date, etc.) was not for me until my children were old enough for me to have the time to prepare. The days go much smoother if Mom is not worried about outside pressures.

What this all boils down to is *learning to set priorities.* There are some things that must be priority items for mothers of young children. Adequate rest is at the top of the list. Time for her husband—and for herself—is vital. A happy relationship with her children is paramount.

> The fatigue of a mother is the single most important element in any family's emotional well-being. If the mother is too tired, she can't be judicious in the treatment and discipline of her children, or give the proper

love and attention to her husband. She suffers and so does her family. The emotional tone of their family life becomes dull, apathetic, inconsistent and irritable.

A mother's fatigue permeates family life in a thousand small ways.[5]

What a child needs most is a lively, lovable mother. If his mother has enough energy to be enthusiastic, enough inner vigor to give off some semblance of a feeling of well-being, a youngster can get along without a lot of other things. Mother's real goal is to see that this need is fulfilled. To do this, she must learn how to keep her inevitable tiredness from getting too far into the fatigue phase.[6]

At the same time I would not suggest that you eliminate outside activities entirely. It is important to have something to think and talk about besides your children. A parent-education program that involves both mother and child (with some time just for mothers to discuss problems and solutions) can be very helpful. Some things you should do all by yourself occasionally (like shopping, visiting a friend, having lunch with a friend). And some things you should do with your husband, like occasional nights out and regular attendance at church. If you are alert to the importance of not taking on more than you can successfully handle, you will soon learn just where your limit lies.

Set realistic goals for yourself. "When a woman can't meet her ideal by accomplishing every self-imposed task," writes Eileen Stukane in a recent issue of *McCalls,* "that's when a sense of helplessness develops. She may wake up each morning hoping that day may be better than yesterday, but by nightfall, when nothing has changed, she is exhausted. If the causes of stress are never dealt with, the helplessness can grow into depression. The depressed woman wakes up fatigued, not wanting even to face the day."[7]

Going to bed with the knowledge that you have not accomplished nearly all you feel needed to be done is frustrating, and ultimately exhausting. Chances are you are trying to accomplish too much, given your particular set of circumstances.

Donald A. Tubesing, an educational psychologist and president of the Whole Person Associates in Duluth, Minnesota, and his associates conduct Stress Skills Workshops across the country. Participants are asked to complete the following statements:

Maybe I don't need to _____ anymore.

Maybe I do need to _____ some more.

Maybe I need to _____ sometime soon.

Maybe I need to _____ once again.

Maybe I need to _____ sometimes.

The first statement clarifies what you would like to change; the second what you want to hang on to. The third is a statement of future goals, while the fourth recalls a resource from the past. The fifth clarifies an area where you need more flexibility.

When Betty Nelson (a wife and mother suffering from the stress of daily living) took the quiz, her answers looked like this: Maybe I don't need to be such a perfect housekeeper anymore. Maybe I do need to develop some more interests outside the house. Maybe I need to find a part-time job sometime soon. Maybe I need to go camping with Billy and Bob once again. Maybe I need to hug them without warning sometimes.[8]

Your priorities and your goals go hand in hand. Once you have established your priorities, your goals will fall into place more easily. Working mothers must be especially careful that they don't assume more household chores than they need to. There's no reason why Dad can't help out. And with two salaries, perhaps you can even afford a cleaning lady once a week. If it means a more rested and happier mother, it will be worth the financial investment.

Exercise and proper nutrition are also important to reduce fatigue. When you're home all day—or working at a job all day—it's easy to let your eating habits slip. But improper nutrition—whether overeating or undereating—will catch up with you, in the form of fatigue and ultimately illness.

I recall reading recently about the mother of quadruplets who had taken up jogging. So would I! It's probably the only time she has all day that she can call her own. Only trouble is I could never figure out when to do it (in the morning, of course) without the children waking up and creating innumerable early morning problems for my husband who is not totally conscious before 10:00 or 11:00 A.M. Jogging at night was out of the question. If I had the energy to move my legs I'd move them into bed, not around the block.

On the occasions when I have indulged in some form of exercise I must admit that it does put new life into the body. "Exercise is one of the best ways to overcome fatigue," says Eileen Stukane. "Expending energy buys energy."[9]

Indulge yourself in the peculiar joys of mothering and providing for the domestic tranquility of your household. A great emphasis has been placed by the women's movement on the fulfillment of working outside the home. Fulfillment as a woman does not come automatically by staying home or by not staying home. It comes through your attitude toward life. If you believe, as I do, that the will of God is at work in your life (because that's the way you want it and you've told Him so), then whatever opportunities come your way are for your good. Some of those opportunities are pleasant. Some are not. Many more are a mixture of pleasure and pain. Fulfillment comes through an attitude of acceptance of and obedience to God's will, and through the peculiar circumstances He brings our way that are suited to our nature. For women, motherhood is one of those circumstances.

I do not particularly enjoy cooking. and the meals I serve are frequently last-minute affairs which I put together in a hurry. (I do try to make them nourishing, but I'm also a master at short cuts.) There are times, however, when I'm in the mood to cook and I plan my menu well. There is an enormous satisfaction in presenting to my family a meal that is attractive, colorful, nourishing—and edible! Especially when I've taken time to enjoy the stirring and the baking and the smelling.

"There are too many times as we go bustling from commitment to commitment," suggests Judith Viorst,

"that we do, for our children, our duty and nothing more. We can't afford just to sit on the floor and help with the jigsaw puzzle. We can't afford to linger too long at night—after all, we've read them their story and we've given them their kiss and it's time to turn off the light and get down to business already. We can't afford a whole Saturday to shop with them for their clothes; we can get it all done Thursday evening if we'll hustle. And often we're like the gardener who will water and weed but forgets about smelling the rose. Smelling roses is hard to fit into our schedule."[10]

Even if we have shucked most of the outside commitments for a while, it's possible to rush through the everyday tasks of mothering and taking care of a house, and fail to enjoy them. There is a deep sense of satisfaction about bringing order to a chaotic dresser drawer, or rearranging a closet so its contents are accessible. There are rewards, no matter how tired we are, in lingering just a moment longer than we might like to at our child's bedside. It's in those quiet moments of alone-with-mom-ness that my children frequently tell me something that's been on their minds. I'd really hate to have missed it.

Slowing down and taking time to enjoy is one of the best ways I know to combat fatigue.

Get to know the ultimate Source of rest. I do not mean to suggest that at our point of greatest weariness God will swoop down and pour new energy into our bodies. What I do want to suggest is that real rest (the absence of chronic fatigue) and peace are interchangeably intertwined.

"Peace I bequeath to you," Jesus told His disciples; "My peace I give to you. I do not give you gifts such as the world gives. Do not allow your hearts to be unsettled or intimidated" (John 14:27).

The troubled heart who is not at peace with herself or with God will never have rest, no matter how much sleep she gets. The world offers peace, just as Jesus said. But the world's peace is a temporary peace often found in bottles and pill boxes. Only Jesus Christ through the cleansing power of His blood can give us lasting peace, "the peace of God, that surpasses all under-standing" (Phil. 4:7).

"Come to Me all you who labor and are heavily burdened and I will rest you," Jesus said (Matt. 11:28). When we confess our sins to Him—sins of short-temperedness, impatience, resentment, bitterness, and a host of others—He forgives and gives us an inner peace that lasts.

Jesus Christ—and the common sense He gives us—are the answers to fatigue.

Notes
1. Dr. Marion Hilliard, *Women and Fatigue* (New York: Doubleday and Company, Inc., 1960), pp. 24,25.
2. Quoted by Eileen Stukane, "Why You're Always Tired (And What You Can Do About It)," *McCall's* Magazine, August 1980, p. 73. Used by permission.
3. Dr. Marion Hilliard, *A Woman Doctor Looks At Love and Life* (New York: Doubleday and Company, Inc., 1956, 1957), pp. 142,143.
4. Ibid., pp. 138,139.
5. *Women and Fatigue*, p. 89.
6. Ibid., pp. 92,93.
7. "Why You're Always Tired . . .," p. 108. Used by permission.
8. Excerpt from "How to Manage Stress," by Jennifer Bolch, *Reader's Digest*, July 1980, pp. 82,83. Used by permission.
9. "Why You're Always Tired . . .," p. 108. Used by permission.
10. Judith Viorst, "Domestic Tranquility," *Redbook*, April 1981, p. 75.

CHAPTER 5

What ever happened
to the woman I married?

Dr. Kenneth Carlson, a Methodist minister and chaplain for the Glendale, California police department, tells of the time he and an officer answered a call from an hysterical mother. Her husband, she claimed, was threatening to kill their newborn child.

Arriving at the couple's apartment, Dr. Carlson and his fellow officer found the woman's husband—a giant hulk of a man—with his arms raised high above his head. His newborn child was in his hands and he was threatening to dash the baby to the floor and kill it. The hysterical mother was cowering across the room.

Sizing up the situation, Dr. Carlson said to the man, "I will give you just 10 seconds to slowly lower your arms and give that baby to your wife, or you will be the sorriest man in Glendale. One—two—three—"

Slowly, slowly, the man began to lower his arms and did indeed give the baby to his wife. After calming the distraught mother and angry father, Dr. Carlson and the officer left.

Once outside, the officer said to Dr. Carlson, "What on earth possessed you to say that to the man? What if he hadn't lowered his arms in 10 seconds?"

"Well, then," replied Dr. Carlson, "I would have extended the time."

His reply was humorous. The situation was not. Why was the man upset? His wife and baby had only been home from the hospital a couple of days. When he came home from work that night, his wife did not have dinner on the table as usual.

The illustration is extreme. Most couples respond with more joy than anger at the arrival of a newborn. But it illustrates the changes that take place in a couple's life when the first child is born. No doubt that father had taken it for granted for many months or even years that when he came home from work, his dinner would be waiting for him. When his entire routine was suddenly interrupted, he couldn't cope. The adjustments facing him were normal ones. However, his lack of maturity prevented him from handling them wisely.

For most couples the arrival of children is a time of great joy. For nine months you have waited and hoped and dreamed. When the child finally arrives, you rejoice in the new life that God has loaned you. You sense for the first time as a married couple what it means to be a family.

In many ways children can strengthen a marriage.

"Having a baby was good for me and our marriage," says Kathy, whose oldest child is now eight. "Before, I was terribly dependent on John. If he was late coming home from work I went into a tizzy. When the baby arrived I had something else to occupy my thinking."

Being a parent gives you new opportunities to work together as a team. Your husband has his work, you have your interests. Now you have children to raise. It is imperative that you be in harmony about how to raise those children. As you talk over the values and beliefs you want to pass on to your children, you open new doors to understanding yourselves as husband and wife.

"Why do you like your daddy, Shana?" I asked our five-year-old the day my husband left on a short business trip.

"I get to play on him," she replied. "He washes my armpits

and it tickles. And he helps me work on my stuff and all."

Her three answers gave me a new appreciation for my husband and his ability to play with his children, meet their physical needs, and share their interests.

Children give a husband and wife an additional mutual concern. Some of our most intimate moments are when we are laughing together over some precious thing our children have done or said.

In spite of how much we love and enjoy our children, their arrival signals a drastic change from our pre-children days. Most of the adjustments we gladly and almost automatically make. Other adjustments take longer and are more difficult. The sooner we make those adjustments the happier we will be as parents and the better we will feel about ourselves as parents, as persons, and as marriage partners.

TIME ALONE WITH YOUR SPOUSE

Even happy family togetherness is no substitute for time alone with your spouse. B.C. (before children) my husband and I could do things together on the spur of the moment. A.C. (after children) even the simplest outing sans children is a major undertaking. Can we afford a baby-sitter? Can I *get* a baby-sitter? Will the sitter be competent? How will the child respond to a sitter? These things were never a consideration before. Now they sometimes look like giant obstacles deliberately designed to keep spouses apart.

"My husband came home one night," says one mother, "and said, 'Hey, let's go out to dinner, just the two of us.' And you know what I did? I burst into tears. The poor man thought he was doing me a wonderful favor—and he was. Except that I was exhausted and we had no baby-sitter and the whole situation seemed too overwhelming to face."

Plan "dates" with your spouse. (Weren't most of your dates before marriage planned in advance?) It takes time to find a baby-sitter and money to pay for one (if you don't have grandparents to occasionally watch the children). But the time spent alone together will be well worth the effort. In a quiet setting with no distractions you can talk in depth. Shouting the day's news over the dinner table din just isn't the same. The day will run much more smoothly if you know you have something to look forward to that night.

Occasional dates are important, but once or twice a year you need *a block of time away* from the responsibility of small children to relax and talk and just have a good time being together. Sometimes we have to hire a sitter for a weekend when the grandparents are unavailable. Rediscovering the things you enjoy doing together is a great strengthening factor for your marriage.

I am especially conscious of the fact that in about 15 years, our children will be grown and may be gone. Once again our home will be filled with just my husband and me. B.C. we enjoyed doing certain things together. In fact, that was part of the basis for our marriage—it made our marriage work. Then along came children—for the next 20 years. If we stop doing the things we enjoy together for that 20-year period, it's going to be mighty hard to pick up where we left off.

We enjoy traveling. For now it may be only a weekend away from the children a few miles from home. But if it is new territory to explore, or a familiar spot we enjoy visiting over and over, it is still travel.

We enjoy going to museums. The children are old enough now that we can begin taking them with us. But once in a while my husband and I sneak off to one by ourselves. We can't do it as often as we used to. But if we make an effort to do it at least once in a while, we will keep the interest and enjoyment alive.

The parent who is totally wrapped up in his/her children is the parent who is going to experience the "empty nest" syndrome most severely. And it's not fair to your mate. Keep doing the things you enjoy—hobbies, gardening, sewing, reading, whatever. And keep cultivating things that the two of you enjoy together.

Another way to achieve some time together is to put the children to bed early. Every family seems to develop its own life-style in terms of the children's bedtime. Some are in bed by 6:30 or 7:00. Others take long naps and are up until 9:00 or 10:00. If you find that you and your husband have no time alone together at all, consider earlier bedtimes for your children. It's important that they be up long enough to spend some time with Daddy when he comes home at night. (When you stop to think about it, the average working father sees his children for only an hour or two a day.) But it may be unnecessary for them to be up until *your* bedtime. TRY skipping the afternoon naps and see what happens. If all you end up with is cranky kids, wait a month or two and try again.

CHANGES IN APPEARANCE

Another factor that can affect marriage is the change in a wife's appearance. After the baby was born, "I gained 15 pounds and I can't get it off," says Cindy, a former model. "Why can't I get it off? Because I'm home all day where the food is!"

That slim, chic woman your husband married may now find herself with stretch marks on her tummy, and extra pounds there and elsewhere. The demands of the children make it difficult to keep up your appearance.

In every office there's at least one woman who's a knockout. Your husband sees her all day long. What does he see when he comes home at night? I say this not to lay a guilt trip on you but to inspire you to action.

It's just as important to keep up your appearance now as it was back in your dating days. Maybe more so. Only now it takes more effort—planning ahead for baby-sitters so you can go to the beauty shop, exercise class, shopping for clothes, or whatever.

B.C. I used to bathe late in the afternoon and dress especially for my husband's arrival home from work. After children, with three preschoolers banging on the bathroom door to get in, or worse yet so small they could not be left unattended for even a fraction of a second, that approach lost some of its pizzazz. A mature husband does not expect his wife to look like a *Vogue* model, but a good hairstyle and a slim figure will do wonders for his morale—and yours.

For those of you with a weight problem, consider this observation by a friend of mine. "Eating," she says, "is one of the few things you can do with small children around that brings pleasure." You can eat sitting down. But you can also eat standing up (if you sit down the children are all over you). You can eat "to keep up your strength until Dad gets home." There are an infinite number of reasons why life with preschoolers can be blamed for your inability to stop eating. I know because for me it's a constant battle.

My children are with my parents in Arizona this week because Grandma and Grandpa want them, they want to go, and I need to work on this book. An instant change in my eating habits has taken place. I no longer crave sweets and bread and all those other fattening things. My nibbles between meals have been largely on fruit or a beverage. At mealtime I eat an average portion. With total peace and quiet surrounding our house, I find no compulsion to eat.

Until the children are in school every day and I have some of that quiet time to myself, eating will probably continue to be a problem for me. But I now have hope that, like other things mentioned in the last chapter of this book, "this too shall pass." (See chapter 7 for more on your appearance.)

MAKING YOUR HUSBAND FEEL LIKE #1

B.C. it was easy to make your husband feel like #1. Now he seems to have slipped into #2 spot, simply because so much of your time and energy must be focused on the children. There's no getting around it. Preschoolers require almost constant attention. There are a few things you can do, however, to make your husband feel the love and admiration you have for him.

Greet him at the door like you're really glad to see him, even if you are ready to drop. "That way he comes in feeling wanted," says 27-year-old Nancy, whose husband is on the staff of a large church. "Everything after that may totally disintegrate," she continues, "but it doesn't seem to matter because he comes into the house feeling like a king."

On occasion my children and I form a rooting team when my husband comes home from work. As soon as he comes in view we give out with a big "Yea, Daddy!" and applaud him for all we're worth. The look on his face lets us know how much he appreciates the small moment of attention.

Do you remember to fix his favorite foods? Do you make sure the clothes he needs for an important business meeting or trip are clean? and buttons in place? It's the little things in life that let us know how much other people care.

MAKING YOUR WIFE FEEL LIKE #1

With the drains on one's self-esteem that mothering sometimes brings, wives need to feel that they are still attractive, still fun to be with, still important to you in every way. Some men have no trouble thinking of "romantic" things to do for their wives. Other men have to work at it. The rewards of a little effort pay off.

Plan a night out with your wife and arrange for the babysitter yourself instead of asking her to.

I accused my husband of buying gifts for me at the last minute (i.e., Christmas Eve) and never planning ahead. (It's nice to know you are being thought about during the day.) I had to eat my words. For my birthday he let the children hide four small containers for me to find. Each container held 25 silver dollars. He had quietly kept a few dollars out of his paycheck each week for several months and exchanged them for silver ones in preparation for my birthday. I was surprised—and pleased.

Last Christmas Anne's husband Ted presented her with a "Christmas Coupon Book" (several small pieces of paper stapled together) which he had made himself. Each coupon specified something redeemable (see pp. 68,69).

CHALLENGES TO YOUR VALUE SYSTEM

With the arrival of children there may be new challenges to your value system.

"When I was dating my husband," says one young mother, "his smoking didn't bother me. I figured if he wanted to ruin his lungs that was his business. But after we were married and our first child arrived, I suddenly found myself telling my husband to 'get that cigarette out of here. I don't want my baby inhaling that smoke.' "

The differences in values between you and your mate may not have been a problem B.C. A.C. you begin to rethink and

This is your

Christmas
Coupon Book

Look for exciting details inside →

THIS ENTITLES

ANNE SMITH

TO (1) ONE LUNCH OUT WITH _TED_

ON A WORK DAY!

SEXESEXESEXESEXESEXESEXESEXE

THIS COUPON ENTITLES _ANNE SMITH_ TO ONE (1)

SHOPPING TRIP FOR $35.—

WORTH OF SEXY* GARMENTS. LUNCH OR DINNER IS INCLUDED
BABYSITTING MUST BE ARRANGED.   *SEXY—feminine, alluring, cuddly,
exciting. Husband must accompany in order to judge whether garments ...

ESEXESEXESEXESEX

THIS ENTITLES

ANNE SMITH

TO ONE (1)

ANNE APPRECIATION SESSION !

reorder the things you feel are important. When values differ greatly between husband and wife, sometimes you will simply have to agree to disagree. It is important, however, that neither of you attempt to undermine the value system of the other. Part of growing up is learning that people—even parents—think differently about things.

YOUR FINANCIAL STATE

Most assuredly there will be changes in your financial affairs. Our financial picture changed not as much when our daughter was born as when the boys arrived. We bought a house in March, the boys were born in July. In November we began a most necessary addition to our house. It has taken us several years to recoup from the financial drain of that year.

B.C. you spent money on yourselves—clothes, vacations, etc.—without too much thought. A.C. you may have to decide who needs new shoes the most—Dad or your two- and three-year-olds. If you both worked B.C., you will also be learning to live on only one income.

YOUR FRIENDSHIPS

As the children come along there will be changes in your friendships. Your old friends will probably remain friends. But you will gradually have more in common with people who have children than with those who don't. Your children will help you make new friends as well. "Hi," says a neighbor, "I'm Susan's mom (dad)." And you've got a new friend!

Don't be afraid to invite single people, elderly people, and couples with no children to your home if they are the type who enjoy children. You all will be the richer for it.

YOUR GOALS

B.C. you set goals and worked at them regularly. Now it becomes more and more difficult to find the time to talk about goals, much less accomplish them. Your husband has his work goals and you have your mothering goals. But it's important that the two of you have some common goals. Think specifically of short-term goals—next summer's vacation, a new chair for the living room, a weekend away for the two of you. And plan some long-term goals—an addition to the house, a financial plan for your children's college education.

"We set five-year-goals," says the mother of two preschool girls. "At the end of each five years we look back and see what we have accomplished."

YOUR SEX LIFE

Privacy is an important part of your sex life. But in a household with preschoolers it's hard to come by. Be there a parent anywhere who has not been at the pinnacle of ecstacy with his/her spouse, only to suddenly realize that a very small pair of eyes are watching everything that is going on. "Suddenly," says one mother, "the body next to me froze."

The remedy may be a simple one: "My husband says he's noticed quite a change in me [regarding their sex life] since we put a lock on the bedroom door."

The need for privacy is another reason for an occasional weekend away from the children. You may find your lovemaking more spontaneous and enjoyable when you know you won't be interrupted by a call in the night or a watching child.

The frequency with which you have sex may change. The nightly nuptials of the newlyweds may give way rather frequently to "Not tonight, dear. I've got a headache (backache, neckache, I'm-sick-of-the-kids-ache)." It is a medical fact that the wife's desire for sex decreases during the first few months after childbirth. If intercourse becomes so infrequent that one of you is unhappy, it may be time to look for hidden causes and take remedial action. It's important to keep every aspect of your marriage alive.

EQUALIZING THE WORK LOAD

B.C. you and your husband could sit together in the evenings and talk, watch T.V., read or what have you. A.C. you find yourself working around the clock doing the hundred and one things that life with children requires. You are scrubbing the floor—and your husband, tired after a day at work, is reading the paper with his feet propped up just like he always did.

Sometimes you feel resentful. It seems so unfair.

Maybe it's time to equalize the work load—*without* feeling guilty. The children are *his* children, too. I do not believe a father can begin to understand what life with preschoolers is like for long periods of time (like all day, for instance), unless he is left alone with his preschoolers for a long period of time (like all day, for instance). Even then, he won't experience all that a mother goes through.

Recently I attended an all-day seminar on a Saturday and my husband was left at home with the children. He enjoys our children and is much better than I at finding fun things for them to do. I knew they'd do fine as they have on other occasions when he's been totally in charge.

When I got home, the day quite naturally had taken its toll on him. "And to think," he said wearily, "you go through this every day."

"That's right," I replied, "except that besides taking care of them I am also trying to cook three meals, do the laundry and keep the house clean."

Fathers and their children must have time alone together. How well your husband relates to children will determine how long he will want to be left alone with them. Some men take to children quite naturally; for others it takes a little time for them to feel at ease.

On a day-to-day basis, it's important that husband and wife work together in this job of parenting. Operating a home for a young family does not mean simply sitting around enjoying our dimpled darlings. It includes washing clothes, changing diapers, making formula, buying groceries, cooking meals, running errands and cleaning house. It's a 24-hour job for one person. When two people share those responsibilities the load is considerably lighter.

Maybe it's time the two of you sat down and planned how you can work together on those responsibilities. Quite naturally, the one who stays home all day is the one who will do the bulk of the work. But a daddy can get up a few minutes earlier in the morning to help dress a child, learn to throw a load of diapers in the washing machine or assume some other chore on a regular basis. The lines of demarcation between what is "woman's work" and what is "man's work" have been challenged in recent years, and, happily, virtually destroyed. Household chores are neither masculine nor feminine. They are simply jobs to be done.

We now have the freedom to choose our own areas of responsibility. A wife needs to know that her husband will consistently do the grocery shopping, arrange for repairmen, clean the living room, or whatever he has agreed to do. A husband has just as much right to know that his wife will faithfully make out the grocery list (before it's time for him to do the shopping), keep clean shirts and underwear in his drawers, and weed the front flower bed. However, these divisions of responsibility need to be flexible. Certainly there will be times of illness, weariness, or special circumstances when one cannot fulfill his responsibility at a given time. But there must be a measure of consistency for a smooth-running household.

COMPLIMENTING EACH OTHER

I bought a new navy blue bathing suit recently. "I really like your new suit," my husband said. "The color helps to minimize the mass." I suggested to him that the term "minimizing the mass" might be fine in the design business, but "it looks more slenderizing" was more acceptable around home. We laughed. And I felt good that he liked my taste in swimsuits.

"You sure have a lot of patience with Michael," or "I really admire your ability to listen attentively when Andrea wants to tell you something" goes a long way toward building self-esteem as a parent. It also helps build your marriage.

TWO KEYS

Perhaps nowhere else are you faced with as much opportunity for growth as in your marriage relationship. The more unselfish you are, the less self-centered, the easier will be your adjustments. The struggles of parenthood can do more to cement the marriage relationship than almost anything else in life. As together you learn, succeed, fail, experiment, and discover the wonderful world of raising children, your relationship will be strengthened. Your love will grow deeper for each other.

There are two keys that will help you unlock the door for growth in your marriage relationship. *One is acceptance of the fact that what you are experiencing as parents is normal and to be expected.* It's the way things are. Sleepless nights, diaper rash, sticky kisses, dirty dishes, finger marks on the walls, pint-size bear hugs, "I love you, Daddy" in the middle of the night are all part of parenthood. The good and the bad flow together in unending succession. And those days will be over too soon.

The alternative is to set the children aside, so to speak, until they are older. Endure, provide, take care of, but without enjoying to the full the child himself and the lessons you can learn from him. With this alternative you only stand to lose.

The second key is to appreciate the commitment aspect of marriage. We were on our way to Grandma and Grandpa's, a horrendously long trip by car with three preschoolers. The children were restless. The boys were fighting. George and I were yelling. Throwing aside all the rules for good parenting, I said to the boys, "Why can't you be quiet like your sister?" (who was lying quietly at the back of the station wagon). A few minutes later we pulled into a gas station and I found out why Shana was so quiet. She was sick—and she proceeded to throw up.

At the point of total exhaustion we staggered into a restaurant for something to help keep our bodies alive. Number 2 son had been unbearable and decided to continue his crabby routine. I decided he wouldn't. With a mighty yank he found himself outside the restaurant, my hand firmly connecting with his bottom. A customer walked by announcing, "Oh, I remember when *I* used to have to do that." (More power to you, lady.) Number 2 son decided crabbiness was not paying off. Back at the table, our daughter collapsed on my lap, too sick to eat.

My husband's eyes and mine met across the table.

"You know," I said wearily, "if it weren't for the commitment aspect of marriage, I'd say 'so long' and be on my way."

With his customary humor, he replied, "And what makes you think I would still be here for you to say 'so long' to?"

Because we are committed to marriage and to raising our children together, there was a bond in that miserable experience that strengthened us.

How long, one wonders, will it take the world to once again return to the belief in the commitment aspect of marriage? Long before there were children, God knew the stresses and strains on a marriage that children, wonderful as they are, would create. He also knew that total commitment to each other as husband and wife was absolutely essential to the healthy growth and development of children and of the family. "For this reason a man shall leave his father and his mother and cling to his wife and they shall become one flesh" (Gen. 2:24). There is no substitute for "clinging" together as an act of total commitment.

Anniversary

For better for worse, Lord,
means that even if the dental hygienist
     with the frosted hair
promises him a free prophylaxis
he'll rinse, please, and head home.

For richer for poorer, Lord,
means that even if my girl friend Doris
promises she won't mind my buying the mink chubby
I buy the dyed rabbit that sheds
and tell him mink is pompous and passe´ and,
     besides, it makes me look old.

In sickness and in health, Lord,
means that when I get anxiety attacks
     he holds my hand
and when he gets sinus attacks
     I hold his head
and when we get intestinal flu simultaneously
we take turns crawling out of bed
     for the ginger ale.

To love and to cherish, Lord,
   means never having to say "Speak to my attorney"
   and till death do us part means what was fine at
   the start of this immense journey
   will do for the end.
   Whatever, Lord
   And amen.[1]

Note
1. Toby Devens Schwartz, "The Anniversary," *Lord, My Husband's in the Kitchen* (New York: Doubleday and Company, Inc., 1981), reprinted in *McCall's* magazine, September, 1980.

CHAPTER 6

I used to be so organized

The dirty dishes were piled higher than the human mind can conceive. It was our first year with twins and a two-year-old and the kitchen was an absolute shambles. By dinnertime I was too exhausted to breathe and had given up living and gone to bed. My husband was just about ready to tackle this mountain of crockery when a neighbor dropped by to bring us some fruit. Now this was not just any neighbor. It was a neighbor whose child is long since grown, whose house is always immaculate, and who likes things done properly and well. There stood our kitchen in all its disastrous splendor.

She didn't say much at the time, but the next day she returned to see if I had gotten the fruit. (Did she think it had disappeared among the dishes?) I really think she came back to see if the house was still standing.

B.C. I always considered myself an organized person. I could usually keep my appointment calendar straight. My house was reasonably clean and uncluttered. The laundry was done before we ran out of underwear. Life flowed rather smoothly.

Then along came three children. For every toy I picked up, three or four replaced it. The laundry still got done, but often at midnight. Until my neighbor asked that I not run the dryer after bedtime. It sounded like a vacuum cleaner through her bedroom window.

And meals were frequently a catch-as-catch-can affair. With a little luck something edible was in the refrigerator when I opened it at 5:00 P.M..

If you were an organized person before becoming a parent, you no doubt have found new challenges for your organizational skills. If you never were very organized, you will need to work a little harder now. While I think it is ridiculous to expect mothers of small children to keep an immaculate house, there is a limit. A house that is constantly a shambles is not a pleasant place to be for either the occupants or visitors.

The first thing to decide is just how clean your house must be to satisfy you and your family. Is an absolutely spotless house an imperative for you? Are you miserable if every dish isn't washed and in the cupboard, every bed made, every pillow straightened? If you are a super neatnik, then you will have to give up other demands on your time in order to maintain such super sanitary conditions. And what often goes is some of the time you could be spending with your children. The neatnik mother must *constantly* be cleaning and picking up (and crabbing at other family members to pick up their things).

At the other extreme, do you worry about how your house looks only when company is coming? Is it hard to walk a straight course through the living room? Has the hall closet not been opened for four months for fear of an avalanche? Have you seen the Department of Sanitation truck cruising by your house for the last week? Have you switched to green plastic food containers so you won't have to see the mold in the refrigerator?

Somewhere between these two extremes we have to strike a happy medium. Trying to be a neatnik will give you (or your children) ulcers. Paying too little attention to your house will never help your children learn how to take care of a home and its contents.

Finding that happy medium will probably mean adjustments and compromises for everybody. Taking care of children requires an enormous amount of time and energy. It doesn't leave much of either of those commodities for anything else.

If your husband insists on an immaculate house, take off on an all-day shopping trip some Saturday and let him care for the children. Be sure formula needs to be made, a load of diapers has to be washed, and at least one meal prepared. Some husbands would draw up divorce papers by the time their wives came home, so be wary. But it is a wonderful way to show the husband who comes home at night and says, "What did you do all day?" a chance to discover exactly what you did!

If your self-esteem as a woman is based on how clean your house is, you may need some professional help. Every mother of young children needs: time with her children, time with her husband, time alone with herself, time away from home, regular church attendance, and some activity (hobby or other interest) that can provide relaxation. If you work outside the home, you have another aspect to juggle as well. Obviously you can't devote all of your time to any one of those things. Your priorities will determine how much of your time will be spent in each area.

Keeping a clean house means constantly balancing all of these activities. If the house is a mess, I may spend more time on it one day than on other things. Another time, the kids and I may do something together that takes the better part of the day—and the housework can wait. Or my husband and I may go somewhere together—and both the house and the kids can wait. Real growth as a parent, I am convinced, means deciding what is important and learning to successfully balance the various aspects of our lives.

ORGANIZING YOUR HOUSEWORK

To simplify housework, *begin by eliminating unnecessary items*. It will take a little time, but it's worth it. Clean out those closets one shelf at a time and throw or give away the things you don't really need.

My boys have somehow accumulated, through assorted birthdays and Christmases, a laundry basket and a plastic washtub full of toy cars and trucks. Before our next garage sale I'm going to sit down with the boys and have them sort those toys (four-year-olds are old enough to make some decisions). We are going to pull out a few to keep, select some to give to an Indian school where Grandma and Grandpa teach; the rest will go to the garage sale. Proceeds from the sale can go into their savings account. Those vehicles take up a lot of space in the closet. No two boys need that many of anything.

Do you really have time to make jam to put in all those empty peanut butter and pickle jars? Or, will you have accumulated even more jars by the time you have the time and energy for such a task? Do you really need five sweaters when you only wear two? Take a realistic look at everything in your house and get rid of what you don't really need.

The next step, now that you have cleaned out your closets and cupboards, is to *have a place for everything*. It makes cleanup easier for everyone, including children. If all the puzzles go on the second shelf, and the dress-up clothes go in the bottom drawer, a child has no excuse for shoving things under the bed because he doesn't know where to put them.

That brings us to my third suggestion: *Include your children in your housecleaning.* Children need to feel that "this is *our* house and we all work together to keep it clean," not "this is Mom's house and we mustn't mess it up or she'll get mad." Children can dust, run the vacuum cleaner, sort laundry and clean fingerprints off the window. They can learn to set the table properly—fork to the left of the plate, knife and spoon to the right. And what young child isn't in seventh heaven when he's allowed to wash the plastic plates and cups in the kitchen sink? They won't be as efficient as you, but I've been surprised sometimes at how much help children really can be.

Children also need to realize that some jobs have to be done before they and you can play, because that's the way life is. Say, "Help me put the clothes away and then we can do what you want to do."

Encourage your youngsters to take responsibility for their own rooms and belongings as soon as they are able. If they get their clothes wet or dirty, they can remove the items, put them in the proper place, and put on clean clothes. If they wet their beds (because they forgot to go potty the night before), let them strip the bedding from their own beds and carry it to the washing machine. They can fold clothes and put them in their dresser drawers.

By the age of five my children are required to make their

own beds. They will not make them as neatly as I would, but that's okay. They are learning. I recall a preschool teacher saying that she always went behind her daughters and remade their beds to make them look neater. One day her girls said to her, "Mom, can't we even make a bed right?" Mom learned a valuable lesson.

Some mothers can get their toddlers to pick up clothes and toys by making a game out of it and by singing little "pick up" songs. If you can do that, more power to you. I usually found it required more energy than I could muster to do it on a regular basis. I prefer to wait until my children are capable of doing jobs with less of my supervision.

Some jobs are obviously beyond a child's capability. And there are times when you need to work alone. Save those jobs for naptime. Or give the child something (such as Play-Doh) to work at in the same room with you. Do the job during a television program the children are watching. Or send them outside for a few minutes with a timer so they know they aren't going to be left out there indefinitely. Lock the door if necessary. When the timer rings, they may come inside. Children must learn reality. They are not capable of doing every job, as much as they would like to.

Make a list of jobs you want to complete by the end of the day or week. My friend Alice says she used to have a particular job in the back of her head that she wanted to work on whenever she got the chance. By keeping it in mind, she was ready to tackle it on a moment's notice.

Ask your husband to help. If the work is piling up faster than you can cope with it, talk with your husband about his assistance. If he likes to cook, perhaps he could take over cooking one meal on certain days, or some of the weekend meals. Dads can easily grocery shop, vacuum, take the drapes to the cleaners, and a host of other jobs. But often they need to be asked. A man who has been gone from home all day cannot read your mind. His ESP doesn't automatically tell him that housekeeping chores need his attention as well as yours.

For households with more than one young child (especially if you have a multiple birth or several children very close together), *let the major cleaning jobs go for a while.* Your first year with babies is terribly time consuming. Your house will not fall down if the walls aren't washed this year. And nobody will see the dirt on the baseboards except you.

Some women are able to afford a *cleaning lady* once or twice a week. A little extra help never hurt anybody.

Set limits. If you entertain regularly, tell your children not to bring their toys into the living room. It's nice to know that at least one room of your house looks acceptable if people drop in. Have a pickup time just before mealtime. Take a lesson from my grandmother who always picked up the clutter before she went to bed. It's a lot nicer to wake up to a clean house than to one that is still messy from the day before.

And certainly you will want to set limits on where food may and may not be eaten. A moldy banana peel at the bottom of the dirty clothes hamper is not nice.

BASIC STORAGE PRINCIPLES
1. Store items at the point of their first use.
2. Stack identical items.
3. Place items at convenient heights.
4. Use dividers to separate items.
5. Place items most frequently used in the most easily accessible places.

ORGANIZING STORAGE SPACE
"How can I be a neat housekeeper," I wailed to a relative one day, "when not one closet in my house is big enough to hold the things that are supposed to go into it?"

Is there a woman anywhere who has enough storage space? To relieve the overloaded closet syndrome at our house, *we bought a portable closet.* Many kinds are available. The one we bought is a brown metal storage cabinet purchased at an office supply store for less than $80. We use it to store toys, games and puzzles in the boys' room. Since children love to crawl into tight places, this cabinet has magnetic catches which prevent them from being locked inside.

I got the idea for such a cabinet from another mother of twins who had one in each of her children's rooms. The one in her twins' room started out holding diapers and baby clothes. She locked hers to prevent curious toddlers from pulling out the contents. The one in her daughter's room went into the back of a closet to hold toys. The closets come in various sizes and colors. If the color doesn't suit, spray paint it to match the decor of the room. It's really adding one whole closet to your house.

Buy or build a toy box. There are two schools of thought about toy boxes. One says, "Avoid a bin to throw things in." Toy boxes are considered poor because things get buried at the bottom and children never learn to place toys neatly on shelves. I agree. But on the other hand, I have to say they are helpful if time is at a premium. During the first couple of years with our two babies, it was a blessing for me to be able to quickly clear the floor of toys. The boys were quite capable of pulling things out of the toy box. And what they didn't see they didn't miss anyway. If you do use a toy box, be sure it is an open box with no lid. Lids can fall down and mash fingers (or heads); also the toddler can climb into an open toy box without having the lid close and trap him inside.

Open shelves are a better way to teach neatness. Whether the shelves are attached to the walls with brackets, or inside the closet, or in a low bookcase, the toys are easily accessible and just as easy to put back where they belong.

Stitch drawstring toy bags of various sizes from denim or heavy cotton. Use them to hold toys with many small parts such as Legos, blocks, small cars, etc. Attach a cup or mug holder to the wall and hang the bags from the pegs. Or attach clothes hooks to the wall or inside of a closet door. Toy bags are also good for traveling.

Brightly colored laundry baskets are ideal for holding large trucks and cars. *Smaller plastic tubs* can hold coloring books and crayons, puzzles, etc. Reinforce the inside corners of game boxes to prevent breakage. A *tall plastic wastebasket* can hold bats and balls, hobby horses, and other tall, tippy toys.

Other storage possibilities. Use the space under the couch or bed for large trays, pictures, and children's art work. The space behind doors is tailor-made for ironing boards and other tall flat objects. Recess shallow shelves between the studs in the kitchen to hold spices, cans of soup and other small items. Build shelves or a closet underneath a stairway. Small buckets or margarine tubs are just right for miscellaneous small objects.

Search magazines and household books for other storage ideas you can use at your house. When I get to heaven, my house is going to have nine rooms of nothing but storage space. (I wonder if God knows about that?)

KITCHEN STORAGE

Organize your kitchen storage into three areas: (1) the mixing center, (2) the range and serving center, and (3) the sink center.

The *mixing center* is where you mix doughs and batters and prepare foods. The refrigerator is part of this center. Cabinet storage should include many of your staple foods such as flour, spices, canned goods, baby foods, etc. Store utensils such as blenders, beaters, mixing bowls, refrigerator dishes, plastic wrap and bags, trays, cutting board, measuring cups, etc.

At the *range and serving center* you perform all types of oven and surface cooking. Supplies stored in this area should include tea, coffee, small amounts of flour and sugar, cooking oil, salt and pepper and spices used in surface cookers, macaroni, rice, etc. Store utensils such as measuring and stirring spoons, spatula, pancake turner, skillets, pressure cooker, kettles, serving dishes and platters.

At the *sink center* you wash vegetables and fruits, slice and peel, drain foods, collect and remove garbage, wash dishes. Store dried foods requiring soaking, vegetables such as potatoes, condiments, detergents and soaps, cleaning powders (be sure these are not accessible to young children, however), and, paper towels. Other items stored at this area can include aprons, clean dish towels, garbage can or disposal, vegetable brushes, can opener, etc.

ORGANIZING YOUR TIME

Basic to household efficiency is the way we handle our time. There are two major time-consuming areas that need careful scrutiny as our children proceed through the preschool years.

Away-from-home activities for children. I have watched with interest (and a measure of dread) as I see mothers suddenly turn into chauffeurs when their children enter the elementary school years. A major portion of the week is spent shuttling offspring from music lessons to ballet and tap to Little League practice and to church activities.

I sampled that experience this summer when Shana was enrolled at Church Discovery Camp for two weeks and Reed and Scott were at VBS one of those two weeks. In a 13-day period I made 25 trips to and from our church (or the park, if that was the pick-up point for Shana). My body was permanently bent in a sitting position, and my fanny was glued to the Naugahyde. "Next year," I said to myself, "I will have several car-pool parents lined up before we try this again."

Does your four-year-old really need cherub choir *and* ballet lessons? Does your kindergartner really need soccer practice on Tuesdays, Bible Club on Wednesdays, and piano lessons on Friday? I am all for giving children the advantage of biblical and musical education, as well as participation in sports. But I also believe they need to have time to just be children. They really don't need everything at once. It is draining on their energy—and on yours. Quality time spent on one activity is enough for most preschoolers.

Outside activities for you. Every mother needs something she enjoys doing besides the house and children. It may be teaching Sunday School or singing in the choir. It may be a hobby such as gardening or crewel work, or attending a class now and then to learn a new skill. Such activities outside the home can help you be a more interesting conversationalist and can relax (or stimulate, if that's what you need) both mind and body.

But like anything else, outside activities can take over your life if you are the kind who finds it hard to say no. I think Christian women are particularly susceptible to becoming over-involved, because we have some mistaken notion that God has called us to serve the whole world. However, if we look at the hidden reasons we take on too many church activities, we may find that our real motives are not so God-centered after all.

If you have great difficulty saying no when people ask your help, ask yourself why. Are you constantly seeking escape from your home and/or marriage? Do you need the ego gratification of always being the person people call on when they need help? Have you learned to discipline your use of time? Or do you let other people set your priorities for you?

We only have one opportunity to be parents. If things start going badly for our children when they hit third grade, we can't turn back the clock and make them babies again so we can start over. If we blow it now, that's it. There are no more chances at being a Christian parent of preschoolers.

It behooves us, therefore, to carefully think through our use of time during these formative years. A child has learned half of all he will ever learn by the time he is three years old, say the child psychologists. And every parent of a three-year-old can attest to that. But who has he learned those things from? Even the best baby-sitter is not a mother or father. Are you too busy to take time for your children?

GETTING YOUR ACT TOGETHER

Make a priority of setting aside one block of time each week for major planning. Make out your week's menu and grocery list. (If I ever do this more than two weeks in a row, my home economist friend who advocates it will fall over. It really works when I do it. But it takes a great deal of discipline on my part to make myself plan meals.)

List all of the errands, lessons, appointments that require your time. See how many things you can combine: drop shoes at the shoe shop on your way to the grocery store; have your husband pick them up on his way home. Write that thank-you note to Aunt Amy while you wait for your daughter at the dentist's office. If the baby-sitter is available for only two hours on Thursday, combine a hair-cut and lunch with a friend at your local department store.

Write appointments on a master calendar. Hang a small chalkboard or an erasable memo pad in the kitchen. Write down all the activities for the day and cross them off as they are finished. You'll feel a great sense of accomplishment at the end of the day to see all those lines drawn through jobs completed.

Keep a sheet of paper on the refrigerator to jot down food items and staples that need replenishing. Some women use a calendar or notebook full of lists and appointments which they refer to throughout the day. Experiment with various types of record keeping to discover which method works best for you.

If you are having serious trouble managing your time, talk it over with the Lord. Anybody who can create an entire universe in six days and still have an entire day left to rest must know how to use His time to the best advantage. Tell Him your problem and ask His help in determining each day what things should be done and what things can go undone. Make a list and ask Him to help you sort out the necessary from the unnecessary. If you trust God to provide the time needed for the essentials, then you need not blame yourself or anyone else for the things that go undone. Perhaps today it's more important that you spend time reading to your sick toddler, and tomorrow there will be time to bake cookies for the bake sale.

SPACE AND TIME, LORD

The earth is the Lord's and the fullness thereof
And I do not begrudge Thee
    the vastness of Thy universe
But, Lord, I need space.
More than the edge of the bed,
the last drawer,
the shared closet,
the bathroom split with the cat
   (not fifty/fifty either, and
    there is litter in my Rive Gauche talc again),
more than the single file in the cabinet,
the hem of the blanket,
the slice of Chevy leather between
    the rock that is my husband
    and the hard place of the baby's car seat,
more than the back burner.
Space, Lord.

And time.
More than the length of a shower,
the run of Sesame Street,
the breath between her last cry for the night
    and her first one in the morning,
more than the tumble-dry cycle,
the hour of co-op nursery,
the shrinking nap,
more than his evening out.

Space before I cannot run to fill it.
Time before I do not care to spend it.
These blessings I ask in Your name, O Lord, amen.[1]

A RESOURCE: *Getting Organized* by Stephanie Winston
(Warner Books) is an intensely practical guide to organizing just
about every aspect of your life. See especially the chapters on
organizing children's rooms and how to handle all the paper that
floods our homes each day. I highly recommend this book.

Note
1. Toby Devens Schwartz, "Space and Time, Lord," *Lord, My Husband's in
the Kitchen* (New York: Doubleday and Company, Inc., 1981). Reprinted in
McCall's magazine, September 1980.

CHAPTER 7

I used to be somebody

Much has been written about the importance of helping children develop good self-esteem. Feeling good about ourselves is a vital part of growing up. We talk about our children's self-esteem in chapters 3 and 10.

Right now, however, let's talk about *your* self-esteem as a parent. How we feel about ourselves as parents determines in large part just how much joy we derive from parenting.

In his book *What Wives Wish Their Husbands Knew About Women*, Dr. James Dobson says that low self-esteem is the most troublesome problem among American women and the cause of frequent depression. Even if you have a good view of yourself, parenting brings with it some new challenges to your self-esteem.

Some of you left promising careers to become mothers. If you were happy with your job, no doubt you experienced frequent back pats that said, "You're doing a good job!" Raises, compliments from the boss, successful financial dealings all tell us that we are doing well.

Then you became a mother and suddenly found yourself in a whole new world where back pats are the exception rather than the norm. Your best efforts at work were usually successful. But here's this tiny child screaming his lungs out for no known reason—and your best efforts to calm him are *not* successful.

At work the amount of time you put in—maybe even over-time—was noticeable, a sign that you were faithful and reliable. You accomplished things. You got jobs done.

At home you work hard all day and at the end of the day the toys have been restrewn across the living room floor, the dinner burned while you were changing the baby. And the laundry is still in a heap on the floor because every time you tried to load the washer the phone rang or the children needed something. To your just-home-from-work husband it is NOT obvious that you have spent a profitable day.

All too soon we realize as parents that we have just been entrusted with the most important job in the world—and no-body anywhere along the line has told us how to do it. Especially how to do it WELL. Our parents served as role models of how parenting should or should not be done. Perhaps we studied child development in college, but we soon discover that much of what we learned has little relevance to what we are experiencing day by day. So we are left to struggle along, doing the best we can, hoping by some miracle that what we are doing is right. That struggle sometimes takes its toll on our self-esteem.

"I'm always pulling up my 'carrot,' " says Nancy, whose oldest child is two-and-a-half, "and saying, 'No, I'm not a good mother yet.' "

Each of us brings to parenting the self-esteem we have developed throughout all the rest of life. If you are a self-accepting person who understands your strengths and weak-nesses, the frustrations of parenthood will be short-lived. If, however, you have serious feelings of self-doubt, the joy of parenting will be harder for you to discover. The better you feel about yourself, the easier you can face the day-by-day chal-lenges of being a parent.

Let's look briefly at some of the things discussed in earlier chapters that can affect a mother's self-esteem.

1. *Your weight.* There's something about motherhood that brings out the pounds in us. For many of us, the battle of the bulge begins with the first pregnancy. It may be the first time in your life you have ever had to worry about what you eat.

2. *Your appearance.* On the job you wore stylish suits and dresses, flattering heels and jewelry. In short, you looked *good.* Then came the mother's uniform: jeans, shirts, simple dresses. Considering the fact that your day consists of changing diapers (with certain inherent risks therein), scrubbing floors, hosing down dirty kids, and the like, your uniform is most appropriate. But glamorous it isn't. Slowly your clothing dollars are being spent more and more on "casual" clothes and less on truly feminine attire. Those weekly trips to the beauty shop, too, drift off into never-never land. In short, it's all too easy to "let yourself go."

3. *Your organizational ability.* "I don't believe I can think two consecutive thoughts," a mother of three told me when her children were small. "I am constantly being interrupted." When my three came along I understood how she felt. "I used to be so organized," I would say as I looked at my house in its usual state of disarray. And the errands I did without thinking twice became monumental tasks when I had to lug along three babies. Constant interruptions make it difficult to carry on adult conversations, think, or finish simple tasks.

4. *Your cooking skills.* You used to enjoy preparing a lovely meal for you and your husband. Now you knock yourself out and the kids say, "Yuk. Do I have to eat that? Can't I just have a peanut butter and jelly sandwich?" You wonder sometimes if they will ever learn that foods come in colors other than brown and red.

5. *Your time.* If you work outside the home, you no doubt wonder if you are spending enough time with the children. Dads, too, sometimes worry about the quantity and quality of time they are giving their offspring.

6. *Your social status.* The women's liberation movement has done a colossal job of diminishing the joys of being a stay-at-home mother. "Raising children and maintaining a home hold very little social status in most areas of the country," says Dr. James Dobson, "and women who are cast into that role often look at themselves with unconcealed disenchantment."[1] In reality, you have been entrusted with the most important job on earth. But the world doesn't want you to know that.

7. *Your children's behavior.* The only time in the last six months the children have been really cranky is the day Aunt Tillie comes to call. What you once thought were your little angels now seem hell-bent in the other direction. If there is anything they can do to upset Aunt Tillie, they do it. And Aunt Tillie, who is not known for her tact anyway, manages to let you have it before departing. Even though YOU know Aunt Tillie is a witch and the children are really NOT like they seemed today, you feel just a little discouraged. Why couldn't I have kept them under control? What did I do wrong?

One mother explains her frustration this way: "My son Andrew bit a child at Sunday School—and *I died.*"

On several occasions I have taken the children to a restaurant alone. When the boys were two, I did it with fear and trembling. (Why not gamble, I figure, if it means I don't have to cook?) Usually things went pretty well, but not always.

Often people would come over to our table and tell me how well behaved the children were. I would beam with the pride of accomplishment and then say, "Thank you." It suddenly occurred to me one day that *I* was taking all the credit. It was my children who were being praised for good behavior, not me. So I began saying to the children, "Did you hear what that nice lady said? She said you acted very nicely. I'm really proud of you." I couldn't help feeling, though, that I too had passed the test.

8. *Your marriage.* We've touched on this before. But it bears mentioning again. You are both so busy with children, jobs and home that sometimes your relationship gets neglected. Then come the thoughts: "I wonder if I'm being a good wife (or husband)." "I wonder if he still finds me attractive."

9. *Your expectations.* How well do you face the realities of parenting? Does your house have to be spotless in order for you to feel good about yourself? Do you feel a failure if your children disobey or get into trouble? Do you expect your husband to be the perfect lover, even though the baby has kept you both awake for the last two nights? Expectations that are too high for your children, your mate, and yourself will only contribute to your feelings of worthlessness when those expectations are not met.

HOW TO GET THE BACK PATS YOU NEED

All of us need encouragement regardless of our calling in life. It's the way God made us. The apostle Paul instructs us to give "honor to whom honor is due" (Rom. 13:7). That means someone has to *receive* the honor being given. It's a two-way street. If you accept a compliment, you give the other person the opportunity to express appreciation. Thankfulness and appreciation are important parts of our growth. If you accept an apology, you give the other person the opportunity to say "I'm sorry" and be forgiven.

Do not feel guilty when people praise you for the way you handle your children. And if there's nobody around to pat your back when you need encouragement, look for somebody to do it—without feeling guilty. You need it in order to grow.

You are not locked into a negative self-image. Poor self-esteem can be improved. On the days when you're feeling discouraged about the job you are doing as a parent, take charge and do something to give yourself a lift. The rest of this chapter suggests a variety of things you can do to boost your self-image.

SHARE THE GOOD TIMES—AND THE BAD— WITH YOUR HUSBAND

One of the most enjoyable times of the day is when I can share with my husband the children's accomplishments for the day. He's just as pleased as I am that Shana got a "happy face" on her reading paper, or that Scott made his bed all by himself, or that Reed's insight into a particular situation was surprisingly mature.

When I've had a bad day, he hears about that too, not only because I want him to know what goes on while he is away from home, but because I need some moral support.

For some strange reason, human beings (and particularly women), tolerate stresses and pressure much more easily if at least one other person knows they are enduring it. This principle is filed under the category of "human understanding," and it is highly relevant to housewives. The frustrations of raising small children and handling domestic duties would be much more manageable if their husbands acted like they comprehended it all. Even if a man does nothing to change the situation, simply his awareness that his wife did an admirable job today will make it easier for her to repeat the assignment tomorrow.

Everyone needs to know that he is respected for the way he meets his responsibilities. Husbands get this emotional nurture through job promotions, raises in pay, annual evaluations, and incidental praise during the work day. Women at home get it from their husbands—if they get it at all. The most unhappy wives are those who handle their fatigue and time pressure in solitude, and their men are never very sure why they always act so tired.[2]

Compliment each other often. And if no compliment is forthcoming, ask for one. "Didn't I do a nice job on Cynthia's dress, dear?" Or, "How do you like the toy truck Billy and I put together?"

"Sometimes I feel like I'm on hold—not really growing," says one mother. "Until my husband says, 'You talked to Timmy very well.' Then I feel like maybe I have grown after all."

SEEK OUT OTHER MOTHERS

The support of other mothers is an important part of child rearing. If your husband makes cracks about how "all you women do is sit around and gab," it's time to educate him. The daily traumas of childhood are much easier to bear if mother has an understanding adult to talk to.

In past generations and in other cultures where several generations lived under the same roof, there was always another adult around. Not so in our culture. Therefore, we must seek adult companionship outside the home. Why shouldn't it be another woman who is experiencing the same things we are? It beats laying it all on the postman.

I shall never forget a sweltering June night when my 20-month-old daughter decided to have a temper tantrum. I was pregnant (in the miserable stage) and my husband was out for the evening with relatives who were visiting from the east. The screams coming from my daughter's bedroom were, I'm sure, penetrating the entire neighborhood.

After checking and double-checking to make sure it really *was* a tantrum, I left her to cry it out. But my head was still swimming with the worries of a new mother. What if there really *is* something wrong with her? What must the neighbors think? I wonder if she is keeping people awake. And then there was a knock at the door.

It was my next-door neighbor, Gail. At first I thought she might have come over to complain that Shana was disturbing her children's sleep. But she voiced no complaint. She simply sat down and stayed with me for almost an hour (until Shana finally gave up and went to sleep). She didn't complain about the noise. She didn't give me a lecture on what to do about temper tantrums. She didn't try to tell me how to raise my daughter. She simply stayed with me at a time when I was alone and upset and not feeling very well. She gave me moral support.

I am grateful for the women friends God has given me. We have helped to sustain each other through our children's preschool years. I called my friend Audrey at 8:30 one morning. "At the rate things are going around here," I said, "I'm not going to make it. Are you coming down or shall I (meaning the children and I) come up?" And on her bad days Audrey would call me for help.

For several years our church had a special program for mothers of small children called "Mornings for Mom." Meetings were held monthly at the church and nursery and child care were provided. For two hours the mothers shared problems and solutions, prayed together, and listened to speakers talk on topics of interest to mothers of preschoolers. Our local college also provides a weekly parent education program for both mothers and preschoolers.

Take advantage of opportunities such as these in your area. There is nothing quite so encouraging as to meet with a group of mothers and discover that "all two-year-olds act like that." It's good to know you are not alone.

LOOK FOR HUMOR

It started out as a simple enough request. My son wanted a hard-boiled egg. I stalled him until closer to lunch time, then delivered the goods thinking happily that the egg would make a good nourishing part of his lunch. He peeled the egg carefully, then asked for a bowl to put it in. No problem. But there was more.

"I want a beater, Mom."

"You don't beat hard-boiled eggs, Scott."

"I want a beater, Mom."

"It's uncooked eggs that you beat with a beater, Scott, not hard-boiled ones."

"I want a beater, Mom." He's not one to give up easily.

"Scott, you don't understand."

"I want a beater, Mom."

"Steven (neighbor boy), would you tell Scott that you don't beat a hard-boiled egg?" The look on Steven's face indicated that a worldly-wise six-year-old knows far more about hard-boiled eggs than a mere three-year-old.

But my three-year-old was persistent.

"I want a beater, Mom."

As one who is keenly aware when I have just lost an argument, I gave him a beater. And do you know what I learned? You can beat the stuffing out of a hard-boiled egg! (And yes, he did eat it.)

Several days later, my other son asked for a grinder for his hard-boiled egg. I matter-of-factly explained to him that you don't grind a hard-boiled egg, you beat it. Then I suddenly heard myself screaming, "What am I saying? You don't beat a hard-boiled egg!" But the battle had been lost long before.

I was watching a mother with small children in a restaurant the other day. Things were not going well for her. She was tense. Her face was tense. Her skin was tense. Even her hair was tense. I understood perfectly what she was going through trying to keep those little ones in tow. If only she could laugh, I thought, her task would be lots easier to handle.

Look for the humor in frustrating situations. It makes the rough days at least bearable.

DON'T COMPARE YOUR LIFE

Don't compare your life now with your life B.C.—especially the freedom you enjoyed then. That was another chapter in your life. In a few years it may very well be repeated (when the children are grown and gone), but not now. You have chosen to have children. Partial loss of freedom is part of the whole package.

DON'T COMPARE YOURSELF TO OTHER MOTHERS

You've all met her somewhere—Supermom. *You* may have had to answer the door with only one of your false eyelashes in place. But not Supermom. Her appearance is always flawless. *Your* house may look like Hong Kong after a monsoon. But not Supermom's. She's organized, efficient. She seems to have all of life's parts hung on the proper hook. But look a little further.

She may be a gourmet cook. But is she *ever out* of the kitchen? Does she have time for her children? It takes time to cook truly elegant meals. Her house is spotless. But is it livable? Does she make life miserable for her family if things are out of place?

Each of us has strengths—and weaknesses. We also have priorities. Whatever you consider most important is where you will invest your time. I do not mean to imply that a woman cannot do more than one thing well. But nobody can do *everything* well.

LEARN PARENTING SKILLS

Learn all you can about parenting. "Parenting is not instinct, it is a learned skill," says Jo Schlehofer in her book *Joy in Parenting*.[3] The more you learn about parenting the easier it becomes. Subscribe to magazines for parents, read the book reviews and book ads and buy or borrow books that look like they might be helpful. Attend classes and seminars for parents offered by your church and community organizations. Just as you were continually learning to improve your skills in the working world, learn all you can about raising children. The more you know, the better able you will be to deal with problems as they arise. And the more skills you develop to deal with those problems, the better you will feel about yourself as a parent.

HELP OTHERS

Helping others helps take your mind off your own problems. Channel the children's energies into making cookies for an elderly person in the neighborhood. Perhaps you can all pitch in and do some simple project for the person, such as raking leaves. It will give you something to do besides sit home and feel tired, and will also demonstrate to your children your concern for others.

ENLIST DAD'S HELP

Enlist Dad's help in teaching your children to show appreciation for what you and others do for them. Although I still hear some "yuks" at the dinner table, I also hear my boys say, "Mom, you're a baker, and a cooker, and a good looker." (They learned part of that from their dad.) An unexpected "Thank you, Mommy (or Daddy), you're really fun" brings joy to the heart of any parent.

RESPECT YOUR SPOUSE

Respect and affection are two cornerstones of good self-esteem. When your spouse treats you with respect, you feel like a person of worth. Children do need to see you hugging and kissing as much as you need to do it. Compliment each other in front of the children and in front of other people. It will do wonders for your ego—and for your marriage.

TAKE TIME FOR YOURSELF

It struck me soon after I became a mother that the parent-infant relationship is the only relationship in the world where two people spend all of their time together—24 hours a day, seven days a week. (There are a few exceptions, I realize.) Mothers and school-age children are apart several hours a day. But mothers and young children must of necessity spend all of their time together—unless a temporary mother substitute (called a baby-sitter) can be found.

This "all-the-time" life-style is normal, but it need not be strictly adhered to. I fear for the later adjustment of the child whose mother is afraid to leave him in anyone's care but her own. A mother also needs time away from her little one. Each of us requires moments with no one but ourselves to think consecutive thoughts, commune with our souls, and to fellowship with our Lord.

"When my children were small," says a pastor's wife who raised four, "a lady in our congregation came over one afternoon a week to take the children out for ice cream. Somehow she managed to keep them gone for about three hours. That's the one thing that got me through the week."

Since our boys were eight months old a wonderful grandmother from our church has taken care of the children on Wednesdays so I can get out of the house and recoup. Knowing I would have one chance during the week to get out from under all the responsibility helped me through many a week. I use the time to shop, have lunch with a friend—in short, RELAX. (For a while I had a part-time job on Wednesdays, and that was good for me too.)

If you think you can't afford a baby-sitter that regularly, think instead that you probably can't afford not to. You will come home wonderfully refreshed and ready to tackle another week.

WORK ON YOUR APPEARANCE

Treat yourself to a new hairstyle and good cuts regularly. Trim those extra pounds. You'll feel incredibly better about yourself when you look in the mirror. If your makeup has not been updated in the last couple of years, visit one of the cosmetic stores that specializes in make-overs. Merle Norman Cosmetics gives free makeup lessons. For a fee, Elizabeth Arden Salons offer a "Visible Difference Day" which includes a facial, new makeup, a manicure and a new hairstyle.

Take advantage of classes offered to help you spruce up your wardrobe. A course called "The Image of Loveliness" taught from a Christian perspective offers eight weeks (one night a week) of instruction. Topics covered include building a basic wardrobe, style and color coordination, ideas on makeup and hairstyles, etc. Write to Joanne Wallace, Founder, Image Improvement, Inc., 1223 Edgewater St., N.W., Salem, Oregon 97304 for the location of a class near you.

I find pants and tops the most comfortable and practical attire for everyday. But sometimes I get tired of the monotony. If I have a reason at all to go out of the house (a trip to the post office will do), I put on a dress or skirt and blouse. I find myself feeling much more feminine.

Once in a while treat yourself to something frivolous—a manicure, a sexy nightgown, a piece of jewelry. You need not spend a lot of money. But the impact will be "I'm special and it's okay to treat myself to something I don't absolutely have to have once in a while."

SET GOALS

One of the best ways to feel a sense of accomplishment is to reach a goal. It may be a goal related to the children such as teaching them to identify colors or to ride a bicycle. Perhaps it's a goal for you and your husband—saving enough money for a weekend away by yourselves. Other goals might include taking a class or developing a hobby. Be realistic about your goals. Don't attempt things you can't possibly achieve in your present circumstance. You'll feel good about yourself when you achieve worthwhile goals.

DEVELOP OUTSIDE INTERESTS

Every mother needs an interest besides home and family. Having something else to think and talk about besides the baby's diaper rash will make you a more interesting conversationalist to your husband and to others. A limited amount of involvement in the church and community will give you a more balanced outlook on life.

VIEW YOUR MISTAKES AS OPPORTUNITIES FOR GROWTH

"When do you feel good about yourself as a parent," I asked my husband the other night, "and when do you feel bad?"

"I feel good about myself," he replied, "when I see character growth in the children, when they begin to develop a conscience. I feel bad when I've failed my family in some way. But I see it as an opportunity for growth."

All of us make mistakes. None of us is perfect. With God's help we do the very best we can. But sometimes we blow it. If we turn to God with our mistakes, He will use those mistakes to show us more about ourselves and also about Him. Our mistakes will then become stepping-stones to greater maturity.

TAKE A NEW LOOK AT YOUR CREATOR

Take a new look at yourself in terms of what God thinks of you. For you can't really know who you are without knowing your Creator. God has made you in the image of Himself. He has designed you for a specific purpose: to glorify Him. He needs you to fulfill His mission in the world. And that mission right now can best be fulfilled through your life as a parent.

I firmly believe that God gives us the specific children we need (with the personalities they have) to help us grow. I also believe He gives children the kind of parents they need to help them grow.

Sometimes He gives us a child in relationship to our gifts. My friend Alice adopted a three-year-old girl who had been severely deprived. Her deprivation was such that she has not yet caught up with her peers in emotional development. Alice's gift is the gift of compassion or mercy (see Rom. 12:8). Her personality is ideally suited to working patiently with a child who requires an enormous amount of time.

At other times He gives us children who will help us develop in a new area. I had always had a horror of multiple births. I used to kid my doctor when I was pregnant with the boys that if he ever found two heartbeats I would change doctors. And he never did find two heartbeats—though he very successfully managed to deliver two baby boys!

It was a very difficult pregnancy and I did not know I was going to have twins. But I remember thinking one day, about two months before the boys were born, "Even having twins wouldn't be as bad as this. At least then I wouldn't be pregnant." I later realized I had turned a real corner at that point, which helped to soften the shock of twins. God was preparing me for what lay ahead, although I did not know it at the time.

We had planned to have *two* children. That's how many we thought we could raise rather easily. But God knew we needed to be pushed and stretched. And having three so close in age has indeed stretched me to the outer limits of my soul! I have had to acknowledge my weaknesses and inabilities and my dependence on God and other people. I have had no choice but to grow. And for that I shall be eternally grateful.

God called my husband and me to raise three children. He has also called you to a task. And because of who He is, He will give us all the help and strength we need. He cares. He never gives us more than we can handle with His help.

The song our children sing at nursery school sums up so beautifully what I've been trying to say in this chapter:

> You are very special,
> There's no one just like you.
> God has made you special,
> There's no one just like you.[4]

Notes

1. Dr. James Dobson, *What Wives Wish Their Husbands Knew About Women* (Wheaton: Tyndale House Publishers, 1975), p. 25.
2. Ibid., pp. 51,52.
3. Jo Schlehofer, *Joy in Parenting* (New York: Paulist Press, 1978), p. 4.
4. Jack M. Averill, "You Are Special," *More Songs for 4's and 5's* (Nashville: Broadman Press, 1978), p. 5.

CHAPTER 8

"Her children rise up... and call her"

There is an unwritten law at our house that at whatever hour of the morning Mother arises, a young child will arise also. No one ever lobbied for this law and the democratic process never saw it put to a vote. It is simply a fact of life.

No matter how quiet I am—be it 5:00 A.M. or 7:00 A.M.—if I arise with the faint hope of accomplishing some task ALONE, within moments a small person will come pattering out of his/her room. And that person will have no intention whatsoever of returning to the warmth of a cozy bed for the last little bit of shut-eye. With a smile of delight to find someone else up also, he/she is ready to face the day.

Because of this seemingly irreversible law, I find little comfort in stories about "women of God" who rose daily before day-break to spend an hour (or more) in prayer and Bible reading. And no one *ever* interrupted them.

I suspect some of the stories have been exaggerated a bit in the telling. But even if totally true, I think I can safely guarantee that the children of these saintly creatures were most assuredly *not* preschoolers. Or if they were, they must have been sent away to boarding school as soon as they were weaned.

I can't recall the last time I had an early morning quiet time.

For that matter I can barely remember the last time *anything* was quiet at our house. Yet I *need* to feel God's presence —especially now that I am a mother. And so do you. We need to keep growing in the Word if we are to share God's love with our children. To continue this closeness with God, as with every other aspect of parenthood, we must readjust our expectations and our priorities.

TALKING TO GOD

Learn to pray on the run. "Here me are," my two-year-old said grandly, announcing his entrance into the family room. Then, perhaps thinking better of his faulty grammar, he corrected himself, "Here *I* are."

As simply and directly as a two-year-old, we can talk to God on the run.

"Here I am, Lord. Thank you that Reed did not have a concussion when he fell off the picnic table this morning, and that I got the paring knife out of Scott's mouth in time. Thank you for the incredible piece of clay 'art work' that Shana brought home from nursery school for my Mother's Day present. And thank you, dear Lord, for a little boy who likes to take time to smell the flowers. Now help me get through the rest of this day, Lord. It isn't even noon yet!"

Paul tells us to pray without ceasing. He does not say where we are to pray, in what position, or even the time of day. He says simply that we should pray.

You may long for a quiet conversation with our Lord. The time for that will come. In the meantime, the children's chatter doesn't interfere one bit with His ability to hear your prayer.

Pray with your children. When our daughter first learned to talk, her bedtime prayers were endless. She could "God bless" more people than any preacher going.

By the time she was about four, however, she lost interest in praying. A "God-is-great-God-is-good-and-we-thank-Him-for-our-food-Amen" delivered at record-breaking speed at meal-time was the best she could do. At bedtime she became giggly and, I think, a little embarrassed, so I didn't push it. But I did insist that she be quiet while *I* prayed.

One evening recently we went shopping together to buy her some shoe skates. The stores at the first shopping mall carried nothing suitable that was within our budget or would fit her. So we drove to the second mall.

As we were getting out of the car I said, "Shana, I think we should pray about your skates. God knows if there are some skates here you should have and He will help us find them."

She agreed, so we (I) prayed that if it was His will we would find the skates. I then explained to her that sometimes God says yes, sometimes no, and sometimes wait because He has something better for us.

The second store yielded the perfect pair of skates.

That night at bedtime I suggested that we had just had a specific answer to prayer and I thought she should be the one to thank God for her new skates. And she did (albeit in a whisper). I hope she was as blessed by that experience as I was.

Listening to a child's prayers can teach us a great deal about ourselves and our relationship to God.

"Sank you, God, for new 'jamas and a new playhouse Daddy built."

Are we thankful for the everyday things God gives us, as well as the big things—the playhouses?

"I'm sorry I broke the dish, God. I didn't mean to do it, Mommy."

How readily do we confess our faults to God and one another?

Pray with your spouse. A few moments spent in prayer together at the end of the day or whenever you can fit it in helps solidify your marriage and keep you in tune with God and with each other.

Find a prayer partner. Perhaps you and a friend could become prayer partners. A quick phone call and a quick prayer might help you through the day or help you resolve a problem.

USING THE MEDIA

If a child is sick and you have to stay home from church, find a good Christian radio or TV broadcast. Often the sick child will be sleeping and you can listen or watch uninterrupted.

I have had my faith strengthened enormously by a particular Sunday morning TV program when I've had to miss church. And when my husband came home I had something exciting to share with him besides the grim details of how many times the baby threw up.

The first three months Pam was nursing her first child she listened to a Christian radio broadcast between 4:00 and 5:00 A.M. "I wasn't especially spiritually oriented at that time," she recalls, "but the music lifted my spirits tremendously."

Or maybe you'd rather read a good book. If time is limited, a short devotional from a book such as *Meditations for New Mothers* by Helen Good Brenneman (Herald Press) will give you something to chew on during the day. While you're nursing your first child (and subsequent children, if older children can entertain themselves), you may be able to read longer portions. Or keep a book (and your Bible) beside your bed and read a few pages or verses just before you drop off.

I've been reading a carefully researched study of the events surrounding the death and resurrection of our Lord. Many times the author's observations have made me think, "Is *that* in the Bible? I don't remember that." And I go searching, enjoying the discovery of some new truth from God's Word.

The chapters are short—only four or five pages. I read them just before I go to sleep. But it's enough to keep me learning and growing.

Reading to your children is another way to help yourself—as well as your child—grow spiritually.

Recently I started reading *The Bible in Pictures for Little Eyes* by Kenneth Taylor (Moody Press) to one of my three-year-olds. It provides a marvelous overview of Scripture, I discovered. My son enjoys the individual stories. I enjoy the consecutive order of the stories into which I can plug additional material that I have learned over the years.

Reading Bible stories will stimulate children to ask questions that may challenge your ability to answer. Do you know where heaven is? Or what our new bodies look like after we die?

Recently a friend was telling her almost-three-year-old about the little boy who gave Jesus his five loaves and two fishes.

"I didn't know Jesus liked tuna fish sandwiches," Kimmy exclaimed in surprise. A new discovery for Kimmy. A fresh insight for her mother into the value of giving Jesus the everyday things of life.

REGULAR ATTENDANCE AT CHURCH

Sunday mornings offer parents of little ones a marvelous opportunity—free baby-sitting for two-and-a-half solid hours! (Not that I think Sunday School is merely a baby-sitting service by any means, but I think you get my point.) During that time you can concentrate on Bible study and worship with *no interruptions.*

Many is the morning I have staggered into our Sunday School class somewhere in the vicinity of starting time feeling as if I had already done a day's work. But with a cup of coffee under my belt, and the fellowship of Christian friends (many of whom are also parents of preschoolers), I find myself wonderfully refreshed and ready to study God's Word.

If your class is not meeting your needs, try another one. If the sermons are not helpful, find a radio or TV minister who is—at a time when your children are in bed.

This section would not be complete, however, without a word about the pre-Sunday School hassle on Sunday mornings. Be there a Christian family anywhere who has not had its share of fights prior to and on the way to church?

Some say it's the devil at work. Maybe. The real problem, I think, is simply the fact that *everybody* in your one-(two if you're lucky) bathroom house is trying to get ready at exactly the same time. You'd have the same hassle if you tried to get ready for a party or a ball game that started at a specific time.

Our best mornings are those when my husband and I share equally the job of dressing our three preschoolers.

A REGULAR QUIET TIME

Some preschoolers sleep later and are better able to entertain themselves when they are awake than others. If yours have this gift, take advantage of it.

Connie, mother of three girls —five years, three years, seven months—has a quiet time during the day. She instructs the two older girls to find a book to read for a few minutes while she spends time alone with the Lord. Sometimes her five-year-old asks to pray with her, or takes Mother's Bible and pretends to read like Mom.

It is comforting to children to know their parents are in touch with God.

UNEXPECTED OPPORTUNITIES FOR GROWTH

It was 12 days before Christmas. My body was weary and my nerves were so-so. It took all the strength I could muster to dress myself and the two boys and pack us off to nursery school.

It was chapel day. The usual quiet of the sanctuary was punctuated by the comments of three- and four-year-old children who couldn't possibly sit still—or keep quiet—for longer than 15 seconds. All they could think about was Christmas!

I sank down on the carpet with the boys, right up in front of the minister. It was time to begin the first song. The simplicity of the children's songs almost moved me to tears.

> My God is so BIG
> So strong and so mighty
> There's nothing my God cannot do.
> My God is so BIG
> So strong and so mighty
> My God can make everything new.
> The mountains are His
> The rivers are His
> The stars are His handiwork, too.
> My God is so BIG
> So strong and so mighty
> There's nothing my God cannot do.[1]

With a deep breath and lots of effort from the diaphragm, we adults struggle through "A mighty fortress is our God, a bulwark never failing." The children say simply, "My God is so BIG, so strong and so mighty, there's nothing my God cannot do."

I would not put down for a moment the majestic beauty of

Luther's hymn. It too can draw us to God. But sometimes the stark simplicity of a children's song can speak volumes.

At the nursery school Christmas program I watched with wonder the children's reenactment of the nativity story. These tiny children—so fresh from the cradle themselves—presented in childish simplicity the Drama of the Ages. No one cared that the back of Mary's headdress said Boulder Dam. What mattered was the simple message they presented. Christ was born!

Opportunities for growth are everywhere, if we are open to them. Something the minister said left a question in your mind. What did he mean by that statement? What did the Scripture passage mean? At your first opportunity (the children's nap time?) go to your Bible. With a good concordance you can learn a lot in a few minutes.

A particular verse stands out in your reading. Write it on a piece of paper and tape it above the kitchen sink. A verse like Psalm 37:23,24; Joshua 1:9; or Isaiah 58:11 (Go ahead. Look them up!) can be a great comfort on a particularly rough day with the kids. Leave the verse up there until you've memorized it. Then put up another.

Some of my friends regularly attend a weekday morning Bible study where they are *required* to do homework. While they are in the Bible study, their preschoolers are being cared for lovingly in another part of the church.

"The leader of my Bible study group," says one mother, "called me every week to see how things were going. We had that contact even when my son was sick and I had to miss one of the studies."

Perhaps now is the time for you and your husband to join a weeknight Bible study or sharing group. Time alone with one's husband usually doesn't just happen. It has to be planned. What better way to spend some of it than by studying God's Word together. You might also want to include dinner out before the Bible study, or coffee afterwards, so you'll have some time together to discuss what you've been studying.

LEARNING FROM OUR CHILDREN

Our boys are look-alike fraternal twins—with distinctly separate personalities. At the ripe old age of two, Reed lays everything on the line. What he thinks and what he feels is what he says. You always know where you stand with him.

Scott, on the other hand, is more reserved. If you try to hug him he's apt to run in the other direction. His speech is not quite as advanced as his brother's, so he sometimes struggles to communicate his ideas. When he has finally exhausted his limited vocabulary, he looks at me hopefully and says simply, "I can't tell." I then put into words what I think he has been trying to say, and he goes happily on his way.

God is like both of those boys. Sometimes He speaks directly to us and tells us in an instant what He wants us to know. A verse of Scripture leaps off the page at us. The words of the minister stick in our mind. Or we are brought to tears by the simple trust of a small child praying, "Sank you God Daddy all better."

At other times God baits us, pulls us gently to Him. The child who giggles constantly during prayer time or seldom seems interested in the Bible story being read to him suddenly asks an unexpected question about God. We are caught off guard. We wonder if we gave the right answer. We determine to find out.

Life is so uncomplicated in the eyes of a child. Just so must our relationship be with God—open and honest, allowing God to speak to us in and through our children, in any way He sees fit.

What a privilege we have to learn of God through the means available to parents of young children. The closer we draw to God, the better the chances that our children will not only "rise up," but will also call us—and the God we serve—blessed.

Note
1. "My God Is So Big." No other information available.

CHAPTER 9

Where two or three are gathered together... it's called a multiple birth

A ll you'll do for the first year is babies," people told us after our twins were born. After a few weeks of doing just that, we decided it was time to do something else besides day and night feedings and diaper changes. We'd plan a family outing. We'd show them we could do something else besides just babies.

The outing we planned was to a marina, about an hour from our home, with shops and restaurants along the water. It was a beautiful sunny day. Never mind that it took untold hours of work to get our family ready. It was a perfect day for an outing.

Immediately upon arrival we discovered that one of our infant sons had messed his pants. And his diaper seemed to have forgotten its intended purpose of confining that mess. Everything his small body came in contact with was soon covered—his clothes, my clothes, and the front seat of the car. It was obvious that this change was not going to be a routine one. My husband hiked across the street to a deserted gas station in search of running water. And we commenced the mop-up operation. Suffice it to say, we had the car reupholstered.

A bit nonplussed, but undaunted nonetheless, we loaded babies into the double stroller, took our toddler by the hand, and sallied forth. The blue sky and the clear sparkling water almost made our efforts worthwhile. We ambled along the boardwalk, drinking deeply of the fresh air and telling ourselves we were having a wonderful time.

At lunchtime we found a vacant table along the boardwalk and the children and I waited for my husband to bring our food. It was then that our toddler daughter decided she'd rather see the boats and ran headlong down the ramp that led to the water. My husband was out of sight.

What does a mother do? Leave two tiny babies to the mercy of strangers at nearby tables and run after her toddler? Or stay with the babies and hope calling to her will do the trick? Fortunately, a kind soul retrieved her before I had time to do much more than leap in panic out of my chair.

But we were having a wonderful time.

On the ride home, what hadn't been done to the car upholstery earlier was finished off by our daughter whose stomach decided it really didn't want lunch after all.

They were right. All you do the first year is babies.

The first year with twins is so hectic I feel a little sad that I had so little time to just *enjoy* my babies. This is the year to take shortcuts, to conserve as much of your time and energy as possible. They are babies such a very brief time. Here are some pointers to help you through the first year with twins.

1. *Don't be afraid to ask for help.* The work load for twins is three or four times greater than for one baby. Unless you have a relative nearby to help you regularly, you probably can't afford not to hire at least part-time help.

A whole host of people paraded through our home that first year—bringing us home-cooked meals, watching the children while I ran errands or slept, doing our grocery shopping. Until the boys were sleeping through the night, we hired a neighbor to spend two nights a week at our house so I could get a full night of sleep. When the boys were eight months old—and I had reached the point of exhaustion—we hired a high-school girl to help after school. (I should have done it much sooner.) A wonderful grandmother from our church comes one day a week so I can get out of the house.

If she had it to do over again, reflects one mother of three-year-old twin boys, "I'd take out a loan, if necessary, to get more help during the first year."

If your twins are your only children, the year will not be quite as hectic. But if you have other small children at home, it will be even more difficult. Don't be afraid to ask people for help.

2. Enlist Daddy's help daily. When twins are born, suggests one author, all preconceived notions of what is man's work and what is woman's work go out the window.

Now is a good time for Dad to learn how to change diapers. (Moms don't enjoy changing messy diapers any more than you do, Dad.) A father who divorces himself from the daily routines of raising a baby misses something special. It is in the intimacies of life (changing, dressing, feeding), not just in the fun times, that a father and his child become close.

Some men find it difficult to take on so-called motherly duties. Someone has suggested the reason for this hesitancy is because a man must learn these things from a woman. He must either take orders from you, or remember how his mother used to care for children. And some men feel threatened by having to learn from a woman.

If this is a problem at your house, don't let it become an excuse. Show your husband once how to feed or change the babies. Make sure the diapers, pins, bottles, etc., are where he can easily find them. Then let him go to it. Don't stand over him and offer suggestions for improvement. Provide time when he can be alone with the children (such as when you go to the grocery store) to do things in his own way.

3. Put the babies on the same schedule. Babies generally set their own schedules for eating and sleeping, but two babies may set two different schedules. I soon learned the value of feeding, changing and bathing both babies at the same time. Otherwise you will be feeding babies constantly right around the clock.

One of the joys of feeding time is being able to hold your

baby close as you nurse or give him a bottle. This becomes more difficult when there are two. I've met a number of mothers who successfully nursed their twins, sometimes even both at the same time! Since ours were bottle-fed, my husband and I tried to keep body contact by sitting on the couch with one baby lying on each side of us up against our legs while we held their bottles. You can also feed them in their infant seats, especially when it's time to start solids.

Keep paper and pencil handy to record feeding time and the amount of food and formula each baby takes so there is no doubt in your mind who has eaten what. When you start solids, using one spoon and one dish (unless they are sick) is much easier than trying to juggle two. A special straw-like device is available that fits inside any size baby bottle. It enables babies who are old enough for high chairs to drink sitting up. Saves having to lay them down at mealtime when it's time for the bottle.

4. *A few special pieces of equipment* are well worth the investment. A *double stroller* is an expensive item, but without it you're really housebound. The face-to-face models are the width of a normal stroller, making it relatively easy to get through doorways and down the aisles of stores. It can also double as a high chair when you go visiting. Some mothers prefer the *collapsible umbrella strollers* which can be attached side by side. If you choose this kind, be sure to select ones that give babies good back support.

Car seats, too, are a must for safety when you travel. Since new models come out frequently, study those available to determine which is the safest, and best meets your needs.

When your twins reach the into-everything-crawler/toddler age, the portable expanding Kiddie Corral will be of help. The one I used expanded from an easy-to-carry 12-inch diameter cylinder to more than 12 feet. (It is also available in 8-foot and 15-foot diameters.) With the Corral you can take your toddlers out in the yard—or into people's homes—without fear that they will pull up flowers or knock over vases.

5. *Don't neglect other brothers and sisters.* Our almost two-year-old daughter had been the star attraction for 22

months when the boys were born. But suddenly her world changed as drastically as ours. Her demands for attention, once met fairly quickly, were now met regularly with, "Just a minute, honey. I'm changing (or feeding) the babies."

I tried to allow some time during the day (often only a few minutes) for the two of us to be alone together. And gradually she began to catch on. One day as I was sitting on the couch feeding the boys, she was particularly persistent.

"Mommy, help me with this puzzle," she repeated over and over and over. Since I was holding two bottles at the time, all I could do was tell her that I could watch her put the puzzle together but I couldn't help. Still she kept demanding my help until in utter exhaustion I set the bottles down and leaned back on the couch thinking, "This is all a mistake. I'm just not cut out for motherhood."

To my delight Shana threw herself across me and exclaimed, "Oh, now it's Shana's turn. I love you!"

Another problem for the other siblings is the amount of attention given to twins. People often stop to admire a new baby, but twice as many people (it seems) stop to admire twins. And they often thoughtlessly ignore the other children in the family. It's a good idea to alert friends and relatives ahead of time when the babies are new to greet your other children first and then the new little ones.

6. *Take time for yourself.* If it's a choice between sitting down and reading a magazine or doing a load of diapers because there will be no clean ones in the morning if you don't, what do you do? The diapers, of course. (Unless, smart girl, you have diaper service!) Yet continually shortchanging time alone for yourself takes its toll.

Unless you have regular help, at best you will only have *moments* of solitude. Make the most of those moments. During her first year with boy/girl twins, Rosalie's husband left for work a half hour before her children woke up. She used that 30 minutes to shower, dress and quietly prepare herself for the day.

7. *Take time for your husband and your marriage.* A small baby strains any marriage. Two babies are a double strain. It's important to remember that you and your husband come first.

Early in the game we initiated Friday nights out for Mother and Daddy. When your anniversary rolls around, suggest to the grandparents that the best possible present would be free baby-sitting for a weekend so you and your husband can get away.

8. *Simplify housework and shopping.* Most people do not expect you to keep a perfect house when you have small children. And those who do simply don't understand. If you cannot afford a housekeeper, simplify housework as much as possible. Eat off paper plates once or twice a day to cut down on dirty dishes. Save major housecleaning chores for next year. By the time your babies reach the one-year mark you'll find yourself with much more time for housework. It's unlikely your house will have collapsed into rubble in the meantime.

Locate the "drive-ins" near you: banks, cleaners, dairies, restaurants. It will give you a feeling of freedom (and save time) if you can handle chores from your car without loading and unloading the babies.

9. *Record each "first" in their baby books as diligently as you did for your other children.* Write things down on a slip of paper as soon as they happen or you may frequently find yourself saying, "One of the twins did such and such—I forget which." Put the papers in a safe place and record them in the baby books when you have more time.

10. *Find another mother of twins with whom you can share problems and solutions.* When you're having a particularly difficult day, it's a great help to be able to call another mother of twins and unload a little. Raising twins is quite different from raising a singleton.

Recognizing the unique needs of mothers of twins, the National Organization of Mothers of Twins Clubs, Inc., was formed a number of years ago. Local chapters meet monthly in numerous areas all across the country. Some of the meetings feature speakers such as pediatricians, psychologists and nutritionists discussing the nature and needs of twins. There is also a clothing and equipment exchange and time to talk over problems with the other mothers. For the location of the club nearest you, ask your pediatrician or write to the MOTC headquarters at 5402 Amberwood Lane, Rockville, Maryland 20853.

11. *Take time to appreciate the wonderful double blessing God has given you.* Watching two babies of exactly the same age grow and develop is a unique experience. Know that you are not a mother of twins by chance. The theme of the Mothers of Twins Club is, "Where God Chooses the Members."

Before I left the hospital with our two tiny bundles from heaven, a kind doctor gave me some mimeographed sheets of suggestions for mothers of twins. The last statement on the last page sums up life for a mother of twins: "You will often wish there were two of you, but you will never wish there were only one of them."

THE BOND OF TWINSHIP

In years past twins were dressed alike and treated alike to such an extent that some twins developed real identity problems. In more recent years the trend is toward encouraging each twin to develop his or her individual personality. The first thing your pediatrician may say to you is "Don't dress them alike."

I followed the new thinking to the letter the first few years with the boys until I discovered that, like other theories about child rearing, not every idea works for every child. I have seldom dressed our boys alike. And they have never asked to be. But some twins, I find, prefer to dress alike.

"I try to pick out different dresses," says a mother of five-year-old twin girls. "But we select one dress for one twin and the other girl says, 'I really like that dress. I want one just like it.' I at least try to get different colors."

Another mother of twin girls says her girls are much easier to handle when they dress alike. "I think it's kind of like the school uniform," she says. "It reduces the competition between them."

I also thought it was a great idea to put the boys in nursery school on different days. That way I could have one home alone with me two days a week, and the one at school would have a chance to pursue his interests on his own. It was a fine idea, but it didn't work. For several months one of the boys protested violently when it was his turn to go to nursery school. About the time I was ready to pull him out of nursery school altogether, I began to come to some conclusions. I discovered that he was not ready to be separated from his brother. When we put them together in the same class, a canopy of utter contentment settled over him. Instead of protesting that he didn't want to go, when I picked him up at the end of the morning he was in no hurry to come home!

Yet in another nursery school class there were twin boys who *should* have been separated and weren't.

There is a bond between twins that probably only another twin understands. At times you may feel shut out by their closeness. At other times they may welcome you into their world.

"Would the twins ever separate?" writes Dr. T. Berry Brazelton, associate professor of Pediatrics at Harvard Medical School in an article in *Redbook*. He continues:

> Should they be pressed to have relationships and independent friendships with other children? Wasn't it detrimental to them to be treated alike, to be constantly confused with each other? Should they be separated in school? These were some of the questions that began to plague the Hansons as the twins grew. When Mrs. Hanson looked for it, however, she saw signs of the twins' own efforts to establish separate identities. . . . She found she could trust *them* to let her know when they wanted to be a pair and when they wanted to be different.[1]

When twins are ready, they will separate on their own. Treat them as individuals as much as possible. But be careful not to stifle their closeness.

The joys and frustrations of twins is beautifully expressed in the following essay by a mother of twin boys:

> Wherever I go with my twin boys, aged 15 months, people ask, "What's it like to have twins?"
>
> Mothers with young babies shake their heads in sympathy as I pass with my two, one in a stroller, the other in a backpack. The grocery clerk, the pharmacist,

---

1. T. Terry Brazelton, M.D., "It's Twins!" *Redbook*, February 1980, p. 84. Used by permission.

the mailman all stop to remark, "Wow! My wife goes crazy with one. How do you do it?"

"I have a helpful husband," I tell them.

Having twins is an educational experience. Here are some of the things a mother of twins learns:

To love old men with canes, the middle-aged ladies, and the children on bikes who rush to open doors for her when her arms are loaded with two babies.

That trimming 40 nails on wiggling fingers and toes wipes out the whole morning.

To understand two primitive languages. For one baby, a sweet yellow-skinned fruit is a "tababa." For the other, it is a "boney." A frozen dessert to one is "kiss keem"; to the other it is "alm bean."

To start every day with a prayer. When she forgets, days go harder.

To do leg-ups with one baby bouncing on her stomach and the other standing on her eye.

To discern the "fingers-caught-in-drawer" cry from the "stolen-toy" cry. Failure to distinguish between anguish and anger means she would never finish the dishes.

To suppress emotion. She can smile at the one who cleverly is blowing his banana to cool it, while at the adjoining highchair a lemonade shampoo is in progress.

To feel alone when she scolds one son and the other buries his head in the carpet and moans.

That each child is wonderful for his uniqueness: one for being a willful imp, and the other for being a clinging cherub.

That the question she once believed stupid, "Which is your favorite?" really is valid though she won't admit it. Her favorite is whoever isn't teething, whoever offers her a grilled cheese from his own mouth, whoever is talking to a bird on the window sill.

To love a brave friend who invites her and her two

toddlers over for the afternoon. When she arrives, the friend leads everyone to an unfurnished bedroom and serves tea on the floor with the door closed.

That she can enjoy a picnic dinner at the park, even after extracting insect legs from one little mouth, and something unmentionable from another.

To make instant decisions. Should she rescue the one who wedged his hand on the wrought iron rail, or grab the one reaching for a paring knife?

That other babies have names, while hers are known as "fat one" and "thin one."

To catch her heart in her throat when she discovers her sons asleep on the floor, thin one sucking fat one's toes.

That it is futile to expect anyone to understand her schedule. Her husband, mother, and helpful friends urge her to take a mere 15 minutes a day for herself to read, play the piano, ride her bicycle. If she *had* 15 minutes, she would take a nap.

That what one baby knocks off the kitchen counter, whether a canister full of flour or a bowl of spaghetti sauce, the other will smear over her new wax job.

To follow, with morbid fascination, wire service stories about quadruplets and quintuplets.

To wake one baby early, so he can sample an uninterrupted hug. To run two different directions at once during a rousing game of "git-choo."

To restrain herself when the bubbly girl at the drug store says, "Ooooo, wouldn't it be neat if the next time you had twin girls?"

To hide her pride and fury when her husband says, "These guys are great! You must really have fun all day!"[1]

Note
1. Patti Cargo, "What's It Like to Have Twins," condensed from *Marriage and Family Living*, 1977, pp. 14,15. Used by permission.

PART II

GETTING YOUR
FAMILY TOGETHER

CHAPTER 10

The dawn of civilization

The process of turning an illiterate, willful infant into a civilized human being is a long, slow process. But it is one of the most rewarding experiences of life. All parents dream of what their children may do and be some day. If the children turn out well, the parents thank God for the blessings bestowed upon them. If the children do not turn out well, the parents are often left with doubts, fears, guilt and a hundred whys.

But this is not a chapter about Why. It is a chapter about How. How to help our children become the well-adjusted, happy, secure, civilized human beings God meant them to be.

CONSISTENT LOVE

It was dinner time and the children were dawdling over their food. I was not feeling well and that, coupled with frustration that after hours of begging for something to eat they were not eating, put me in a very bad frame of mind. So I started in on them, expressing my frustration, even slamming my hand on the table for emphasis.

When I had finished my angry diatribe, a small voice beside me said quietly, "When anyone does that, it makes me nervous." Now there's a child who knows how to take the wind out of his mother's sails. All I could do was laugh. (It's hard to stay on top.)

But it isn't hard to love. God knew what He was doing when He made young children. What parent can resist the unexpected hugs, the adorable words and deeds that come as a total surprise, the incredible ways children have of tugging at our heartstrings. The one thing that saves young children from total annihilation at the hands of their parents, I have often said, is the fact that they are so doggone cute!

It's easy to love them, but it's not always easy to show them that love when they do things that get on *our* nerves. What children need most from us is consistent love. A love and respect from their parents that they can count on, no matter what.

Consistent love does not compare one child with another. ("Why can't you play ball like your brother?") It does not withhold itself because a child is bad. ("Mommy won't love you if you do that.") It loves each child exactly as he is, regardless of what he does. It does not love the wrong he does. But it never stops loving the child.

Our example for this kind of consistent love is God Himself. He created us to love Him and have fellowship with Him. And He never stops seeking that fellowship and showering us with His love. The Bible says His love is "everlasting." There's nothing more permanent than that.

When we respond to Him in love, He loves us. When we turn our backs on Him, He still loves us. His love is unconditional and absolutely consistent. That's what makes our relationship with Him so wonderful—and so unique.

CONSISTENT DISCIPLINE

Discipline is what you do for and with your child. Punishment is what you do to him.

There are three major approaches to discipline. The first is the *authoritarian approach*. What Dad and Mom (especially Dad) say is law. There is no questioning and very little discussion. Children are supposed to obey their parents and the wrath of the gods comes down on them if they don't.

There are times when children need to obey instantly (getting out of the way of a moving car, for instance). But most of the time they need to know *why* they are not to do something. They need to know that their actions can hurt other people, cause damage, or make people feel bad. It's part of becoming a responsible human being.

The opposite approach to discipline is the *permissive parent* who lets the child do just about anything he wants. Somebody somewhere dreamed up the idea that the family is a democracy and each family member should have equal say. That is absurd, because young children have neither the knowledge nor the wisdom to know what is best for them. The family structure is a hierarchy with the parents in charge until the children are grown. Without this hierarchy there will only be chaos.

The middle approach holds that the ultimate goal of discipline is to *teach control from within.* To help the child learn how to decide for himself what is right and wrong and to stick with those convictions. The parent who follows this approach is more permissive than the authoritarian parent and more strict than the permissive parent.

Whichever approach you take, consistency is extremely important. And it is often difficult to achieve. You have spanked your toddler's hand twice for pulling the cat's fur, but the third time he does it you are so tired you don't care what happens to the cat as long as you don't have to move. You're tempted to just let it go. But your child's need for consistency makes you follow through.

Children need consistent limits. Their whole beings cry out for it. They want to know what they can do and what they cannot do. And they want you to stick to your guns. They will fight you for control, but they don't really want it. They want to know you care enough about them to control their bad behavior, until such a time as they are capable of controlling it themselves.

Consider for a moment the teenager whose parents allow him to stay out as late as he wishes, use the family car whenever he wants it, pretty much do as he pleases. When questioned the parents will say simply, "Oh, we trust him." What they think is trust, however, is simply neglect. That teenager is as neglected by his parents as if they had abandoned him. Because in essence they have removed themselves from caring about where he is and what he is doing under the guise of "trust." Even a truly trustworthy teenager wants to know that his parents care enough to set limits. Because he knows he is not yet totally in command of his thoughts, his emotions, and his actions.

> [A] child is fully capable of discerning whether his parent is conveying love or hatred. This is why the youngster who knows he deserves a spanking appears almost relieved when it finally comes. Rather than being insulted by the discipline, he understands its purpose and appreciates the control it gives him over his own impulses.[1]

> When a child behaves in ways that are disrespectful or harmful to himself or others, his hidden purpose is often to verify the stability of the boundaries.[2]

Consistency does not start when our children are teenagers. It begins when they are toddlers. Granted, there are times when all of us are too exhausted or too busy with something more important to follow through. But those times should be minimal. If we care enough to be consistent, we will make the extra effort, even when we don't feel up to the challenge.

TIME ALONE WITH EACH CHILD

As an only child I have a rich heritage. I never had to compete for my parents' time. They were always there when I needed them, always ready to listen and care. Certainly, I missed some of the benefits of having brothers and sisters. But I also had much to make up for it.

Every child deserves to be an only child once in a while. He needs some times when the rest of the world is shut out and he has his parent or parents all to himself. At our house we sometimes pre-plan such times. But most of the time we simply seize opportunities. My husband is going to the hardware store, so he takes one of the boys with him. I pick up Shana after school on a day when the boys are with a baby-sitter and we go out for ice cream.

If opportunities for aloneness are not happening, it may be necessary to plan them. Dad can take one of the children to McDonald's for breakfast. Mom and Dad can take one child out to dinner or to the park. Often the oldest child gets to go places with Mom and Dad because the other children are too young. Make sure the younger ones get equal time.

Spending time alone with a child says to the child, "I think you are important enough to want to be alone with you. I like you. I want to be with you and hear what you have to say."

YOUR UNDIVIDED ATTENTION

When I was a small child, my father used to sit on the side of my bed at night and talk to me about the world situation. I understood practically nothing of what he had to say. And my mother used to scold him for talking over my head. But it didn't matter to me one bit. Because my daddy was giving me his undivided attention.

My father is more comfortable around older children than around younger ones. So he talked to me about things he would discuss with an adult. The important thing was not how well I understood what he was saying, but that he cared enough about me as a person to discuss with me what was important to him.

It's not easy to focus completely on your children because so many things are competing for your attention. At breakfast there's the morning paper. A father going off to work needs to be informed about world events. But children need a good start for the day, too. When the child calls, if Dad can look up from his paper immediately and answer the child fully before going back to his paper, it lets the child know Dad cares.

When one of our sons was beginning to talk he had a terrible time getting the words out. He would stammer and stutter, and in his hesitation one or both of the other children would butt in and start talking. This only compounded his frustration and he would cry out in anger. So I learned to stop all three of them and tell them they must take turns speaking and be quiet when it was not their turn. When given the unhurried opportunity and my undivided attention, he was then able to verbalize his thoughts and ideas.

When your child wants to tell you something, get down at his level so you can look each other in the eye. Focus your attention on him and what he is saying. The results will be rewarding for both of you.

HELPING CHILDREN FEEL SPECIAL

One of the most important things a child can carry with him through life is the knowledge that his parents like him just the way he is and think he is very special.

"Do you know," I said to Scott one day, "you are very special. There's no one else in all the world just like you."

"Yes, there is," he replied.

"Who?" I asked.

"My [twin] brother."

"Your brother looks like you," I said, realizing how easy it was for him to feel like an entity. "But he isn't you. You are different and you are special."

How can you make your children feel special? Here are just a few ways. You will think of others.

Take lots of pictures. One family took pictures of each of their children beginning with Mom when she was pregnant with the child, fixing up the nursery, photos of the child's birth, birthdays, etc. Each birthday they show the pictures and reiterate how much Mom and Dad were looking forward to that child.

When the first child is born we take hundreds of pictures. But after the novelty has worn off, we sometimes forget to take pictures of the other children. Make sure you record on film each of your child's special days.

Praise your children often. Praise them for big things and for little things that may seem insignificant. Do not say, "You did a good job" if they are not yet capable of doing a good job (and they know it). Instead say, "You are really working hard. I'm proud of you." Some days it seems like all I do is scold—don't do this; don't do that. It's important to look for the good things they do and reward them verbally.

I used to wonder if I could praise my children so much they might never realize that they still have a sin nature and need to trust Jesus as Saviour from sin. I have learned not to worry about that as long as we are teaching them both sides of the picture. On more than one occasion I have praised a child for his behavior and heard him say, "But sometimes I do bad things." They know. And I look forward to the day I can be sure they have responded to God in the light of that innate knowledge.

Make a flag or banner for each child. I am indebted to author Joseph Bayly for an idea we are planning to implement in our family. When his children were growing up, they made a flag or banner for each child with pictures or words to symbolize that child. On each child's special days—such as birthdays, graduations, special awards, etc.—they hung the banner outside the front door for the whole neighborhood to see. We're making ours out of colored felt. We've checked a book (available at public libraries or bookstores) that lists the meaning of names and plan to attach an item that symbolizes the child's name.

Record their achievements for posterity. On a sheet of notebook paper I record special events that occur throughout the year. At the end of the year I read it to our family to see how much we have grown and matured during the year. Some of the entries for this year include:

> *February 5*—Shana learned how to tie a bow.

> *March/April*—(I describe a 2000-mile trip we made to see relatives in the east.)

> *April*—Reed made his own bed for the first time.

> *April*—Scott was very sick with stomach cramps and nausea for over a week. In the middle of the night he told me if he put his "pinkie" finger up that was his signal that his tummy was okay. That became our hand signal. Pinkie up? Tummy okay.

> One day he called to Mrs. Douglas when he heard his stomach gurgling. "I hear a baby in my tummy," he said. "Oh, boy, we're gonna have another kid!"

> *May*—Shana started piano lessons.

> *June*—Scott learned how to pump on the swing.

> *July 28*—The boys celebrated their fourth birthday with a trip to the fire station as part of their party. Shana discovered her first loose tooth today.

> *September*—Daddy worked very hard for two

weeks painting and preparing the family room for carpeting. Yea, Daddy!

If the good Lord's willing and the typewriter doesn't collapse, I will record for November that Mommy finally finished this book!

Hang a bulletin board in a central place (kitchen, family room, den) and display the children's art work and projects. Let them know you care about what they make and do.

Save some of the projects (first attempts at writing their name, pictures, etc.). When I was a child just learning to color within the lines, I colored a picture very carefully. My mother praised me for my good work—and she saved the picture. That meant a lot.

GIVING CHILDREN RESPONSIBILITY

The best (and only) way for children to learn to be responsible is to be given responsibility. At first those responsibilities are small: putting away one toy before taking out another, placing dirty clothes in the hamper before getting into the bathtub, setting the table. Along with the responsibility they must also experience two things: the freedom to fail and to make mistakes, and the results of assuming or failing to assume the responsibility.

For example, if the child refuses to put away the first toy, then he is not allowed to take out the second one. If he puts his clothes in the hamper without being reminded, he is praised for remembering. If he has trouble remembering the exact location for the knife, fork and spoon he is not criticized for his stupidity.

Sometimes children are eager to help. Capitalize on those times and praise them for their efforts. At other times they need some incentives. Use a wall chart with stars or stickers for each job they complete. A chart completely filled with stickers might win them a trip to the ice cream store.

Giving children responsibility helps them feel a part of the family. As soon as they are old enough, let them have a say in the rules that govern your family. Children will sometimes surprise you with the just ways they suggest for dealing with problem situations.

SEX EDUCATION

Sex education starts with the attitudes we as parents bring into our marriage. Do you view the human body as a marvelous creation of God? Or as something dirty and not to be discussed? Is there warm and open affection between husband and wife? Or is intimacy in every form displayed only behind closed doors?

When our children are very tiny they learn about sex by the way we talk about their bodies. Do you teach your children the correct name for each part of their bodies? Or do you use "nicknames" that are often heard on the street?

Answer children's questions directly when they ask them. A three-year-old child who asks where babies come from does not need to know the whole story because he wouldn't understand it anyway. A simple answer such as "a special place in Mommy's tummy" (not to be confused with Mommy's stomach) will usually suffice. Be careful not to tell them things that will have to be unlearned later (such as "the stork brings babies").

A good place to start is with a carefully-illustrated book written for preschoolers. Concordia Publishing House publishes a series of books on sex education for children through teens written from a Christian perspective. The book for preschoolers (ages five through nine) is titled *I Wonder, I Wonder*. I have used it with my four-year-olds. Because of the length of the book I only read part of it at a time.

Understanding and accepting our sexual identity is an important part of self-esteem. Help your children understand and appreciate the miraculous body God has given them.

GOOD MANNERS

Part of the civilizing process is learning good manners. Children need to learn that the basis of good manners is found in the Bible:

Be kind, Ephesians 4:32.

Whatever you would have people do for you, do the same for them, Matthew 7:12.

Love your neighbor as yourself, Matthew 22:39.

A book I have found very helpful is *A Child's Book of Manners* by Ruth Shannon Odor (Standard Publishing) which explains in a brief text with excellent illustrations how to have good manners at home, at the table, at school, and at church.

The reward for using good manners is that people like us better. Our children need to realize that when they display good manners, they are usually amply rewarded with praise.

HAPPY MEMORIES

What kind of memories do you have of your childhood? I remember the bicycle my parents bought me for my eighth birthday. We had just returned from a long trip, but my parents knew how much that bicycle meant to me. We went right to the bicycle shop to make the purchase.

I remember the time my grandmother wanted to buy me a set of luggage (or some other expensive gift). I was a teenager and thought Grandma's idea was really neat. But my mother talked me out of it. She said it was important to my father to be able to buy me nice things, and since he couldn't afford to buy the items right then, it might hurt him to have my grandmother buy them. I tried to argue the point. But I learned a valuable lesson.

I remember Sunday evenings around the fire when we popped popcorn and listened to Jack Benny and Charlie McCarthy on the radio.

For the most part I have very happy memories of my childhood and for that I am grateful.

> Everyone needs a storehouse of precious memories that enhance a sense of belonging, a sense of being loved, a sense of worth, a sense of competence. A memory becomes valuable as it relates to one's needs being met. The opposite is also true—unpleasant memories are the product of situations when one's basic needs were not being met.
>
> A memory is a legacy—something special, handed down from one generation to another. It can be much more than a material object. In fact, the best memories are often stored only in the mind, not in the cedar chest or the far corner of the attic.[3]

Some time ago I read a suggestion to the effect that we

should consciously try to create happy memories for our children. That is not to say we should (or could) spare them from everything that is unpleasant. But rather that we consciously think through our life-style to see just how much happiness we are putting into our homes. It also means sometimes specifically planning certain things that will bring pleasure to us and to our children.

I realize we cannot second-guess which memories our children will retain. I remember things my parents may have forgotten. I have forgotten things my mother wishes I remembered. But over the long haul we need to make a conscious effort to keep our home life positive.

TRADITIONS

One of the sources of happy memories is traditions. Did you ever think of them as an important part of growing up? Traditions give us a sense of continuity, the feeling that we are part of something special.

I recall the preschool teacher whose daughters were in their twenties but still spending Christmas at home. One Christmas the record player that always played Christmas carols during tree-trimming time was not working. One of her daughters was actually in tears because "we *always* play music when we trim the tree." The happy memories associated with that particular tradition were something she did not want to give up.

For the last few years we have invited my husband's out-of-town sister and her family to share Thanksgiving dinner with us. We see each other briefly at other times of the year, but this is a special dinner we all look forward to. Our children are delighted for a chance to be with their cousins.

At Christmas some families make a birthday cake for Jesus complete with candles. The cake can be eaten by the family or given to someone else.

Tobi and her son Brian make gingerbread cookies and take them to *his* friends and several older people.

Think about the traditions in your family. Which of them is most meaningful to you? Which do you want to continue with your children? What new traditions do you want to start?

A delightful book chock-full of ideas is *Building Happy Memories and Family Traditions* compiled by Verna Birkey and Jeanette Turnquist (Fleming H. Revell Company).

INTRODUCING OUR CHILDREN TO JESUS CHRIST

Our greatest joy as parents is to see our children choose to enter the Kingdom of God. Some people maintain that preschoolers are too young to make such a decision. Others (and I am among them) believe they are not. At least some are capable. I was very young when I committed my life to Christ. I made the decision based on the amount of knowledge and understanding I had at the time. I remember the time very clearly. God has honored that decision through the years.

Every child is different. Some will respond at an early age. Some later. The important thing is that we establish a climate in which they can, by the leading of the Holy Spirit, respond to the claims of Christ when they are ready.

"I had little option in the matter of becoming a Christian," says the well-known British New Testament scholar F. F. Bruce. "The truth of the gospel was the major premise of all thinking and living in the home into which I was born. When I came to years of discretion, I naturally had to make an independent commitment to it. *But it never occurred to me to do anything else*" (italics added).[4]

Establishing that kind of a Christian home should be the goal of all of us.

Notes
1. Dr. James Dobson, *The Strong-Willed Child* (Wheaton, IL: Tyndale House Publishers, 1978), p. 38.
2. Ibid., p. 30.
3. Verna Birkey and Jeanette Turnquist, comps., *Building Happy Memories and Family Traditions* (Old Tappan, NJ: Fleming H. Revell, Co., 1980), © 1980 by Verna Birkey and Jeanette Turnquist. Used by permission, pp. 9,10.
4. "A Man of Unchanging Faith, An Interview with F.F. Bruce," *Christianity Today*, October 10, 1980, pp. 16,17. Used by permission.

CHAPTER 11

What can I have to eat?

It's five minutes after breakfast. Or two hours until lunch time. Six o'clock in the morning. Or one minute after bedtime. Be it day or night, hot or cold, indoors or out, the cry is the same: "What can I have to eat?"

Food is children's most intimate attachment. They like it warm and cold. Sticky, gooey, sweet, sour, mostly eaten with the fingers, inevitably dribbled down the chin. Food gives strength to their tired bodies, life to their growing bones, and direction to an otherwise boring day. "I want a snack" becomes the password of the day.

Food is also their ultimate weapon. They will argue over it. "I'm not going to eat that casserole, Mom. It will make me throw up."

They will try to manipulate you because of it. "Kathy's mother doesn't make her eat rutabagas. And neither does Tim's. Why do I have to?"

They will negotiate over it. "If I eat the beans, can I leave the squash?"

If push comes to shove and they are made to eat both the beans *and* the squash, they will hold the hated items in their mouths chipmunk style for two or three days, refusing forever to swallow.

It is their ultimate weapon, I say, because they *know* you will make them go to bed at night, brush their teeth, get up in the morning, and wear their boots in the rain. But they also know you are *not* going to pry their little mouths open and force the food down their throats. In this one area, they've got you. (Or so they'd have you believe!)

To arm yourself for the food foray, you need to have a realistic idea of what kinds and how much food children really need to eat.

Children eat several small mini-meals, rather than the traditional three large meals. They have no concept of the necessity for eating all of their meal so that in an hour they won't be hungry. It's much more reasonable to them to eat a bite or two now, some more later on. There's nothing wrong with that—except that Mother may soon feel like she is operating a short-order diner.

Any change in routine can affect a child's eating habits: the first week of school, Grandma and Grandpa coming to visit, a vacation away from home.

School started last week (first grade for Shana, nursery school for the boys) and the boys nearly drove me mad. Every five minutes they were in the refrigerator or begging for something to eat. By the end of the week, as I watched them at the dinner table, it finally dawned on me that they were so keyed up they couldn't settle down long enough to eat a regular meal. Consequently, they were hungry all day long.

Last spring we took a two-week trip east to visit relatives. For the first week my three hardly ate a bite, and there were frequent complaints of stomachache. No wonder! They were having a marvelous time and were happy as larks. But they were adjusting to travel in their own way—by not eating. I expected them to keel over. But they didn't. After about a week, they rediscovered food.

The growth of new teeth can also affect their eating habits. "Scott will probably have trouble chewing meat for a while and don't be surprised if he drools," the children's dentist told me at Scott's three-year-check up. And that's exactly what happened. If I hadn't known what to expect, I would probably have been on him to finish the meat his not-quite-in molars prevented him from chewing.

Some children will eat anything in sight, though I've never met one. Most children, however, are picky. Some of their objections to food may be attempts to manipulate you, but at other times their reasons may be valid. Some foods are too spicy for young children. Some have textures that are unpleasant to their mouths. One of the few foods I grew up never learning to like was avocado. And the reason was not so much the flavor as the texture. I did not like that mushy feeling in my mouth. In later years I have learned to like avocado. But as a child I did not.

Another reason children may rebel against eating certain foods is because Mother tries to force them. My grandmother (my father's mother) was, like many of our mothers and grandmothers, pushy about food. She was from the old school that says you really should have "one more piece" or "just one more serving" even when you're full. (If your guests eat heartily, that means you're a good cook.) My father lived in this atmosphere when he was growing up. As a result, he continues to have difficulty enjoying food.

Others of us were taught to "clean your plate. Just think of all the starving children in China (Armenia, India, wherever) who have nothing to eat." Our stock under-our-breath answer was usually, "Okay, I'll send them mine." If the motive behind this admonition was to teach us not to be wasteful, the goal was a worthy one. But the means of achieving it is questionable. It is far better to put less food on a child's plate in the first place than to force him to eat what he does not need or want.

Some children may be picky eaters for reasons that defy explanation (at least to our medically untrained minds). The son of a friend of ours ate nothing but peanut butter and bananas for an entire year. Each time my friend took him to the doctor she would say, "He's still eating only peanut butter and bananas. What shall I do?" Each time the doctor would tell her not to worry about it. Eventually he began eating other foods.

Children's appetites often correspond to their growth spurts. They may be ravenously hungry for a while and then seem to have no appetite at all.

They can miss a meal—and never miss it. Or they can eat you out of house and home. Their bodies are pretty good indicators of what foods they need and how much.

Research in recent years has indicated that adults who are obese often were obese as children. And as often as not they were encouraged to overeat by their parents. Some doctors urge mothers to start their babies on cereal when they are only a few weeks old. (Happily, the current trend is away from this.) Why we are obsessed with forcing infants and children to eat is a question with which we must all come to grips. Forcing children to eat can only lead to obesity and/or extremely negative feelings about food.

But they have to learn good nutrition habits including learning to eat a variety of foods, you say. And you're right. It's how we go about teaching them to eat good food that makes the difference.

My mother tells me she was allowed to eat whatever she wanted when she was a child. And, like any child who is left entirely to his own desires, she wanted a few things, and *didn't* want a whole lot of other things. She recalls a time during her teen years when she was invited to the home of a boyfriend for dinner. There was not one item of food at that meal she liked. Consequently, the dinner was an unhappy ordeal. She made up her mind then and there that she was not going to put herself through that kind of unpleasant situation again. She was going to teach herself to like different foods. But, she says, although she eats many different kinds of food today, she doesn't really enjoy many of them because she never learned to like them as a child.

Somehow we have to strike a happy medium. At our house the "one bite" rule works best. Each child is required to eat one bite of each food placed on his plate. One bite of anything is not overwhelming to a child (though they may give you a stiff argument that it is. A friend tested her daughters by giving them each 10 peas and offering them a chocolate bar if they ate all 10. "I wanted to see if they could eat a vegetable without gagging," she says. They did—and they didn't gag.) After a series of "one bites" over a period of days or weeks, it is rewarding to watch a child suddenly discover that he "likes" the new food and wants more!

Occasionally I relax the "one bite" rule—when there's company, for instance, or we're at someone's home for dinner. Kids—and Moms—need a break once in a while.

One school of thought says that as long as children are eating the right foods all day long, they need not be forced to eat regularly scheduled meals along with the adults. The other school of thought frequently says things like, "No more snacks, dear. It's too close to dinner time. The snack will spoil your appetite." Each of us has to decide for ourselves which approach works best for our family. I opt for some semblance of normal mealtime if for no other reason than that may be the only time during the day we are all together as a family. I usually have a cutoff point for snacks before dinner. But even that doesn't guarantee the children will be hungry at mealtime.

Whichever approach you take, most children still need frequent snacks throughout the day. To keep from spending all of your time in the kitchen, analyze what foods you want them to eat throughout the day and keep a supply ready. I'm referring, of course, to the Basic Four Food Groups: (1) vegetables and fruits (four or more servings of fruits and vegetables of all colors); (2) dairy foods (two to four servings of milk and all-milk products); (3) meat (two or more servings of meat, fish, poultry, eggs, dried beans and nuts); (4) breads and cereals (four or more servings of breads, cereals and macaroni products).

BASIC FOOD GROUP SNACKS

Vegetables and Fruit:

Fill a container with celery and carrot sticks, cherry tomatoes, whatever else is on your child's approved list. Occasionally add a new vegetable until it catches on. Some children like dips. Make a vegetable dip with yogurt as a base and they will also be getting some milk.

A bowl of apples, bananas, bunches of grapes, whatever fruits are in season

Dried fruit. Yes, I know it's expensive. But the entire bag doesn't have to be eaten in one sitting. Ration it out.

Fruit juice Popsicles

Little boxes of raisins (for economy, save the boxes and refill from a larger box)

Small cans of fruit juice (with a straw!)

Dairy Foods:

Individual cartons of yogurt

Individual cheese and cracker snack packs

Yogurt pops (Freeze flavored yogurt in Popsicle trays. For less sugar, use plain yogurt to which you add honey and fresh fruit.)

Individually wrapped cheese slices (fun for little fingers to unwrap)

Meat and Other Protein Products:

Lunch meat slices

Cubes of leftover meat or poultry

Tiny chicken drumettes made by separating the drum from the tip and center of the wing. Fry or bake and keep on hand in the refrigerator.

Nuts and seeds

Peanut butter. Let them make their own peanut butter sandwich or fill celery sticks. Remember that peanut butter is an incomplete protein. Add a glass of milk to make it complete. When I get cries of protest over the milk, I sing a little chanting song: "Milk and peanut butter go together."

Hard cooked eggs

Breads and Cereals:

A slice of whole grain bread. Some kids like to eat it plain.

Crackers of all kinds. A mixture of peanut butter, dried milk and ground raisins makes a great graham cracker sandwich.

Enriched, fortified cereals (My children love to have their own plastic snack bag full of cereal, nuts, raisins, etc.)

Popcorn

Pretzels

If your children are too hungry to last until dinner, give them small bites of the items you are having for dinner: raw carrots that are to be cooked, cheese bits for casseroles, bites of salad.

Do not serve desserts as snacks. Children need to know that cake, cookies, ice cream, etc., are desserts, not snacks.

For a while one of our boys sometimes got so tired by late afternoon he became quite unreasonable. He would cry and fuss and ask to do something that made no sense at all. I watched this happen a few times and wondered what to do. A nurse friend helped me tie his behavior to food.

"If you give a child a piece of fruit for a snack," she said, "all it does is stimulate his digestive juices and make him hungrier. Along with the fruit he needs a little protein." The next time Scott had a "fatigue attack" I tried giving him a snack that included a few nuts. The extra bit of protein seemed to help. In his book *Improving Your Child's Behavior Chemistry,* Dr. Lendon H. Smith suggests a possible explanation for Scott's behavior and the behavior of children who are seldom hungry at mealtime. He begins his explanation with a typical statement by a mother: "Twenty minutes after dinner he claims he's hungry. I ask him why he didn't eat more at supper. He says he wasn't hungry then." Dr. Smith answers:

> If he was hungry for supper about an hour *before* it was offered, his blood sugar might have dropped to a point that would give him symptoms—headache, nausea, vomiting, irritability, depression—that would prevent him from eating, the very activity he needs to correct the cause of his problems. He would be labeled neurotic, rotten, and stubborn, or get spanked or sent to bed for disobedience.[1]

While much of Dr. Smith's book deals with children with special problems such as allergies and hyperactivity, it is no surprise to any of us that food (and also food additives, such as red dye) seriously affect the way all of us think and feel. It is important to feed our children the best possible foods to help them grow and develop and to help them function as well as possible throughout the day. If your child presents unreasonable discipline problems, is hyperactive or frequently ill, Dr. Smith's book could be of help (after you have consulted your pediatrician, of course).

Much has been written about the importance of eliminating sugar and junk foods from children's diets. While I have avoided the extreme of removing all sugar from my children's diet, I do try to eliminate as much as possible. Helping our children develop a taste for foods other than sweets and foods that provide only empty calories is a rewarding experience. It's one I hope will carry over into later life.

Some parents use sweets as a reward to gain acceptable behavior from their children. There is a real danger in this both physically and psychologically.

If you are really concerned about your child's eating habits, consult a book on children's nutritional needs to learn precisely what children need. Then chart exactly what your child eats (meals and snacks) for one week and compare it to his actual needs. If there seems to be a problem, consult your pediatrician. Set ground rules with grandparents, relatives and friends in whose home your child visits as to what he may and may not have to eat.

One of the biggest items in a child's diet is cereal. (Twenty million TV commercials can't be wrong.) Following is a list of cereals calculated according to total sugar content by the Nutrient Composition Laboratory in Beltsville, Maryland, a facility of USDA's Science and Education Administration (SEA). (See the key to the symbols and initials at the end of the list.)

Those cereals at the top of the list contain the least amount of sugar; those at the bottom the most. If sugar is listed as one of the first three ingredients in any canned or packaged food, beware. Ingredients are listed in order of the amount included in the food. And remember, it may be listed by names other than "sugar," such as corn syrup, dextrose (corn sugar), corn sweetener.

In addition to the sugar calculation, I have also indicated the number of grams of protein per serving of most of the cereals (as indicated on the box). A child ages one-three needs 32 grams of protein a day, 40 grams for ages three-six. A bowl of cereal with 6 grams of protein coupled with a slice of whole grain toast (another 6 grams) gives a child a good start for the day. And, of course, there is additional protein in the milk which goes on the cereal.

CEREAL	SUGAR CONTENT	PROTEIN GRAMS
Puffed Rice (QO)	0.1%	1
Puffed Wheat (QO)	0.5%	2
Shredded Wheat (N)	0.6%	2
Cheerios (GM)	3.0%	4
Wheat Chex (R-P)	3.5%	3
Corn Chex (R-P)	4.0%	2
Rice Chex (R-P)	4.4%	1
Kix (GM)	4.8%	2
Post Toasties (GF)	5.0%	2
Corn Flakes (K)	5.3%	2
Special K (K)	5.4%	6
Grape Nuts (GF)	7.0%	3
Rice Krispies (K)	7.8%	1
Wheaties (GM)	8.2%	3
Total (GM)	8.3%	3
Concentrate (K)	9.3%	
Product 19 (K)	9.9%	2
Buckwheat (GM)	12.2%	3
40% Bran Flakes (GF)	13.0%	3
Grape Nuts Flakes (GF)	13.3%	3
Team (N)	14.1%	2
Life (QO)	16.0%	6
Bran Chex (QO)	17.6%*	3
Fortified Oat Flakes (GF)	18.5%	6
All Bran (K)	19.0%	4
Corn Bran (QO)	21.0%*	2
100% Bran (N)	21.0%	3
40% Bran Flakes	21.0%*	3
Life, Cinnamon (QO)	21.0%	6
Most (K)	21.0%*	4
Quaker 100% Natural (QO) (Brown Sugar & Honey)	22.0%	
Country Crisp (GF)	22.0%	
Heartland-Coconut (P)	22.0%	
Familia (BF)	23.0%	

CEREAL	SUGAR CONTENT	PROTEIN GRAMS
Vita Crunch-Regular (OM)	24.0%	3
Honey Bran (QO)	24.6%	
C.W. Post-Plain (GF)	25.0%	
Quaker 100% Natural	25.0%	4
Nature Valley Granola (GM) (Cinnamon & Raisin)	25.0%	3
Heartland-Raisin	26.0%	
Frosted Mini Wheats (K)	26.0%	3
Cin. Frosted Mini Wheats (K)	26.0%	3
Vita Crunch-Raisin (OM)	27.0%	4
Vita Crunch-Almond (OM)	28.0%	4
Quaker 100% Natural (QO) (Raisin & Dates)	28.0%	3
C.W. Post (GF)	28.7%	3
C.W. Post, Raisin (GF)	29.0%	3
Raisin Bran (K)	29.0%	3
Nature Valley Granola (GM) (Fruit & Nut)	29.0%	3
Cracklin' Bran (K)	29.0%	2
Golden Grahams (GM)	30.0%	2
Raisin Bran (GF)	30.4%	3
Country Morning (K)	31.0%	
Graham Crackos (K)	31.7%*	2
Honey & Nut Corn Flakes (K)	31.7%*	2
Cap'n Crunch (QO) (Peanut Butter)	32.2%	2
Cocoa Puffs (GM)	33.3%	1
Honey Nut Cheerios (GM)	35.2%*	3
Crispy Wheats, Raisin (GM)	35.2%*	2
Trix (GM)	35.9%	1
Frosted Rice (K)	37.0%	1
Honey Comb (GF)	37.2%	2
Alpha Bits (GF)	38.0%	2
Body Buddies (GM)	38.8%	1
Count Chocula (GM)	39.5%	
Cap'n Crunch (QO)	40.0%	1

CEREAL	SUGAR CONTENT	PROTEIN GRAMS
Cookie Crisp, Oatmeal (R-P)	40.1%	
Crazy Cow, Strawberry (GM)	40.1%	
Quisp (QO)	40.7%	
Sugar Frosted Flakes of Corn (K)	41.0%	2
Cookie Crisp, choc. (R-P)	41.0%	1
Lucky Charms (GM)	42.2%	2
Fruity Pebbles (GF)	42.5%	1
Cocoa Pebbles (GF)	42.6%	1
Cocoa Krispies (K)	43.0%	1
Cap'n Crunch (QO) (crunchberries)	43.3%	1
Cookie Crisp, vanilla (R-P)	43.5%	
Frankenberry (GM)	43.7%	
Frosted Rice Krinkles (GF)	44.0%	
Corny Snaps (K)	45.5%	
Crazy Cow, choc. (GM)	45.6%	
Waffelos (QO)	45.8%*	2
Super Sugar Crisp (GF)	46.0%	2
Sugar Corn Pops (K)	46.0%	1
Froot Loops (K)	48.0%	2
Apple Jacks (K)	54.6%	1
Sugar Smacks (K)	56.0%	2

* Calculated from label

QO	Quaker Oats	GF	General Foods
N	Nabisco	K	Kelloggs
GM	General Mills	P	Pet
R-P	Ralston Purina	BF	Bio-Familia
		OM	Organic Milling

If your children are not yet happily eating vegetables, camouflage them. Grate carrots (or grind carrots, celery and cabbage) and add to lemon Jell-o with a small can of crushed pineapple.

Following are some additional ideas:

ZUCCHINI BREAD

1 cup oil	2 eggs
1½ cups sugar	2 cups grated zucchini
2 tsp. vanilla	

Beat the above ingredients well. Sift together, then add:

½ tsp. nutmeg	1 tsp. soda
½ tsp. baking powder	3 cups flour
2 tsp. cinnamon	1 tsp. salt

Mix well and add ½ cup chopped nuts, if desired. Bake at 350 degrees for 1 hour in greased loaf pan. Makes two standard size loaves (9 x 3 or 8 x 5).

CARROT COOKIES

2 cups flour	2 eggs
½ tsp. baking soda	1 tsp. vanilla
½ tsp. baking powder	2 cups rolled oats
¼ tsp. salt	1 cup finely shredded carrots
1 cup shortening	(2-3 medium)
1 cup packed brown sugar	1 cup chopped nuts
¾ cup flaked or shredded coconut	

Mix well flour, soda, baking powder and salt; set aside. In large bowl beat shortening, sugar, eggs and vanilla until creamy. Stir in flour mixture, oats, carrots, nuts and coconut. Drop by rounded teaspoonfuls one inch apart on greased cookie sheet. Bake in 350 degree oven 18-22 minutes or until lightly browned. Remove to racks. Cool. Store in airtight container up to two weeks. Makes about 78.

Here's a **Spaghetti Sauce** with many vegetables:

½ lb. ground beef	1 (16 oz.) can whole tomatoes
2 carrots finely diced	1 (6 oz.) can tomato paste
1 green pepper diced	1 (1½ oz.) envelope
1 small zucchini diced	spaghetti sauce mix
1 very small eggplant, peeled and diced	1¾ cup water

Brown meat in large skillet. Drain off excess fat. Add carrots, pepper, zucchini and eggplant. Cook for 10-15 minutes, stirring occasionally. Add remaining ingredients. Bring to a boil. Cover and simmer 30 minutes, stirring occasionally.

NOTE: To camouflage the vegetables, sauté the vegetables separately in a little oil, then whir in the blender when the vegetables are soft. Add to the browned meat and continue. This way no one sees any strange little pieces of vegetables they dislike!

CARROT BRAN BREAD

2 cups whole bran cereal	1 tsp. salt
1 cup sliced carrots	2 cups whole wheat flour
½ cup sour cream	1 tsp. soda
½ cup light molasses	4 tsp. baking powder
1 egg	1 cup raisins (optional)
1 tsp. cinnamon	½ cup chopped walnuts (optional)

Grind carrots in blender with water to make 1½ cups of carrots and juice. Combine with bran in a large bowl. Let stand until bran absorbs moisture. Stir in sour cream and molasses, egg, cinnamon and salt. Beat in flour, soda and baking powder until smooth. Fold in raisins and nuts. Turn into well-greased 9 x 5 loaf pan. Bake 1 hour at 375 degrees. Cool 10 minutes, then remove from pan.

Slice thick and eat with butter or cream cheese. May also be toasted. Refrigerate to keep several days.

Here are some additional snack recipes that combine whole-some foods in an appealing way:

ROCKETS

Cut bananas in half. Insert a Popsicle stick in one end. Roll in honey and sesame seeds or chopped nuts and freeze.

MINI CHEESE PIZZAS

1 tube (8 oz.) refrigerated buttermilk biscuits
1 cup shredded mozzarella, cheddar or swiss cheese
1 cup spaghetti or tomato sauce
oregano to taste

On greased baking sheet flatten each biscuit with floured bottom of glass to 4-inch circle, forming rim around edge. Spread with sauce, then sprinkle with cheese and oregano. Bake in 425 degree oven 10 min. or until edges are lightly browned. Save any left over, covered, in refrigerator up to 4 days. Reheat if desired. Makes 10 pizzas.

PEANUT BUTTER BALLS

1 lb. peanut butter   ⅓ cup honey
1 cup dry milk   ⅓ cup molasses
¼ cup wheat germ

Combine and form into balls.

MOM'S KNOX BLOX

1   3 oz. pkg. orange gelatin
1   3 oz. pkg. lemon gelatin
2 cups hot water
4 pkg. Knox gelatin
    Dissolve, then add:
1   6 oz. can frozen orange juice (undiluted)

Place in shallow dish and chill until firm. Cut in squares.

FRUIT BALLS

1 pkg. dried apricots
1 small box dates
1 box pitted prunes
1 orange
½ box raisins

Grind together, roll into balls and let harden.

PRUNE PEANUT ROLL

1 cup finely snipped, pitted prunes
½ cup chunk-style peanut butter
½ cup light corn syrup

Combine above. Gradually add ¾ cup nonfat dry milk and ½ cup powdered sugar. Mix well and form into a long roll. Roll in chopped peanuts, if desired. Chill until firm. Slice to serve.

POLLYANNAS

2 Tbsp. plus 2 tsp. cooking oil
¾ cup unsifted flour
1 mashed ripe banana
⅓ tsp. baking soda
⅓ cup sugar
⅛ tsp. salt
⅓ to ½ cup pine nuts or shelled toasted
  sunflower seeds

Mix together and dip by teaspoonfuls onto greased baking sheet. Bake 12 minutes at 350 degrees.

Note
1. Dr. Lendon H. Smith, *Improving Your Child's Behavior Chemistry* (Englewood Cliffs, NJ: Prentice Hall Inc., 1976), © 1976 by Lendon H. Smith, M.D. pp. 96,97. Used by permission.

CHAPTER 12

What to do until Dad gets home

There are two hours in every weekday that mothers dread. As the day wears on those hours loom on the horizon like a giant sun refusing to set. Those hours are the two hours preceding dinner and Daddy's arrival home.

The children are tired—and probably bored. And you are definitely tired. Patience is short, tempers flare, tears may flow freely. While it's impossible to eliminate all of the stress during this period, it is possible to relieve some of it.

First, let's look at some of the causes. The children are tired because they have been playing non-stop all day long. Younger ones may have had a nap, but they've still been busy.

They are also hungry and perhaps a little bored. It's a long time since lunch and they're tired of playing with their toys—and maybe with each other!

There is also, I think, an underlying feeling of anticipation because Daddy is coming home soon. I look forward to his coming. I'm sure our children do also. (Sometimes children are *not* so anxious to have Daddy come home, however, because it means they will no longer have Mommy's undivided attention.)

The best way to get through this time period is by being prepared.

PREPARING FOR THE LATE AFTERNOON SLUMP

The most important preparation for the late afternoon slump is rest. Find some time during the early afternoon when you can put your feet up or lie down for a while. If the children nap, nap with them. Four o'clock will look a lot better if you aren't absolutely dead on your feet.

Give the children a nutritious protein snack in the middle of the afternoon—and one for yourself also. A cup of coffee may also give you an extra lift.

Get dinner under way early in the day. Cooking when you are tired and the children are cranky is no picnic. Save some preparation jobs that they can do before dinner—grating cheese, chopping carrots or snapping beans. If you haven't had time to prepare dinner ahead, fix as simple a meal as possible. This is not the night for a gourmet feast. On days for which there is no hope, we often end up eating out.

Have a backlog of simple activities to fall back on if the children are bored and restless. The first place to start is with a Rainy Day (or any day) Fun Box. It would make an ideal baby shower gift, although the new mother would not really appreciate its value for several months. Here's how to make one:

Rainy Day Fun Box. Select a fairly large box and cover it with brightly colored wallpaper, gift wrap or contact paper. Put the items listed below in the box, and any others you might think of. Keeping all these items in one place will save your having to hunt them and will provide hours of fun for your preschoolers.

> Blunt-nosed scissors (sturdy metal ones, not cheap plastic that break easily and/or won't cut well). Have one pair for each child, plus one or two extras for friends.
> Glue or paste (washable)
> Colored construction paper
> Drawing paper (scraps from Daddy's office, a scratch pad or a cheap package of typing paper). Contact a local print shop to purchase end rolls of paper.
> Water colors and brushes
> Crayons (large ones for smaller toddlers)
> Cellophane tape

Colored stickers, stars, etc.

Pencils or colored marking pens

Coloring and/or painting books (for toddlers try the "Paint with Water" books)

Play dough. Buy some or make your own. To make: 1/3 cup salt, 1/2 cup flour, 1 tsp. salad oil, vegetable coloring, enough water to make a bread dough consistency (1/3 to 1/2 cup), 4-6 drops of oil of cloves or wintergreen. Mix salt, flour and water to consistency of heavy dough. Add oil, mixing thoroughly. Add coloring. Store in airtight plastic bag or jar.[1] Provide some cookie cutters and small rolling pins.

Lettering and numeral stencils for older pre-schoolers

Preschool readiness activity books for four- and five-year-olds.

Magazine stickers that come in the mail advertising magazine subscriptions.

A magic slate

Chalk (both white and colored)

THINGS TO DO AT HOME

Make a book. Give the children a pair of blunt-nosed scissors and a stack of magazines. Let them cut out pictures and paste them on sheets of paper to make a "book." You may learn something about your child's emotional development by the kinds of pictures he selects.

When children need some direction, suggest that they cut out pictures of food or animals or different types of vehicles.

Provide a snack. To stave off pangs of hunger my friend Nancy has a mandatory snack time at her house no later than 3:30 (dinner is at 5:00 or 5:30). For snacks she gives them nutritious foods such as apples, cheese and crackers.

Read books. This is a good time to read to the children unless, like I, you tend to fall asleep when you sit down at this time of day.

Give them a bath. Another friend gives her children a bath before dinner. This has a calming effect and also makes before-bedtime less of a hassle. If you can manage it, a bath will relax *you* also.

Watch TV. Somewhere along the line the networks must have gotten the message that good children's TV programs are needed at certain times of the day. In our area "Sesame Street" comes on right after breakfast, which enables me to dress and clean up the breakfast dishes while my children are occupied. At 4:30 in the afternoon "Mr. Rogers" comes on for the second time in the day, followed once again by "Sesame Street" or "Emergency One" (if they've already seen "Sesame Street" in the morning).

Cartoons are acceptable at our house, but I've found it's a good idea to sit down and watch a few once in a while. Occasionally I see one or two that need a comment from Mom.

When my children are especially tired, I ask them to get their pillows and blankets and lie on the floor to watch TV for a while. When they have revived, they often get up and go do something else.

Try an experiment. (1) Pour some vinegar in a small pop bottle. Put a few teaspoonfuls of baking powder into a balloon with the aid of a funnel. Place the balloon over the top of the bottle. Presto! The gas formed by the combined ingredients will inflate the balloon.

(2) A "Mr. Rogers" TV program sent my children scurrying to the kitchen to try this experiment: Fill a cereal bowl half full of water. Sprinkle pepper on top. Dip a bar of soap in the water. The film produced by the soap will push the pepper to the sides of the bowl. Remove the soap. Now sprinkle sugar on the spot where there is no pepper and the sugar will pull the pepper back where it was.

Measure and sift. Give the children a bowl of flour, a sifter and measuring cups. If you don't want the mess in your kitchen while you are preparing dinner, set them up outside at the picnic table (weather permitting).

Rotate toys. Rotate the children's toys. Every three or four months go through the toys and put some of them away in the closet. On a restless afternoon pull out a box of toys the children haven't seen in a while. It will be like getting something new.

Plan a party. When my children visited their grandparents last summer, they planned a party for the retired adults in the neighborhood. They helped make homemade ice cream and my mother taught them the proper way to serve each adult the refreshments provided. "Be sure and invite the Sneffs," said Reed. (Their name is Neff.) And everyone had a wonderful time.

Draw a city. Cover a table with a large piece of butcher paper. Secure the edges with masking tape. Let the children draw a city using crayons or marking pens. Assign each child a part of the city or something you would see in the city. (Talk about skyscrapers, hotels, hospitals, parks, buses and cars.) You can choose other topics as well: a farm, a forest, things you see at the beach.

Special toys. Have a special bag of toys or puzzles that you bring out only before dinner.

String things. Many different items can be found around the house for stringing: buttons, circle-shaped cereal, macaroni. For colored macaroni, place a handful in a jar and add a few drops of food coloring. Cover the jar and shake well. Spread on a flat surface and let dry. Nylon fishing line works best for stringing, but yarn or very heavy thread can also be used.

Make cornstarch dough. Add a small amount of water to cornstarch for a very unusual type of dough. Experiment with the amount of water until you get the right consistency. It appears hard on a plate, but melts from body heat when you pick it up. When the children are tired of playing with it (or if you add too much water), add some food coloring and cook the cornstarch in a double boiler for a different type of play dough.

Finger painting. Place a small amount of finger paint in a strong clear pastic Ziploc bag. Children can squish the paint around inside the bag without getting hands and table messy. In lieu of finger paints you can use catsup and mustard.

Pouring water. Outside in warm weather give the children a tub of water and pitchers, cups, spoons and other containers. Water has a very soothing effect on children.

Invite company. Invite another child over to play. Sometimes the problem of boredom is resolved if there is someone else to play with. If the problem is that there are too many neighborhood children, send them home if you feel your children need to rest.

Listen to tapes. Buy an inexpensive tape player and let the children listen to tapes. Superscope has an entire series of Bible stories and also a series of fairy tales. You will find others at your Christian bookstore.

Tape their voices. If your tape player is also a recorder, let the children tape their own voices and play them back. By about the age of three children can learn to operate a tape recorder.

Sort buttons. Keep a supply of buttons and let the children sort the buttons by color and put them in baby food jars or egg cartons.

Try the high chair. Put your toddler in the high chair near you while you are preparing dinner. Give him a puzzle or book to look at. He will be happy if he can be near you. You will be happy if he is not underfoot.

A surprise box. Prepare a surprise box with things to do only while Mommy is preparing dinner. Place a hand puppet in the box and let the puppet show the children what to do.

Have a puppet show. Collect or make puppets and let the children put on a puppet show for each other or for their friends in the neighborhood.

Plan a surprise for Daddy. Plan a special surprise for Daddy—a picture they have drawn or painted, some leaves collected from the backyard, an impromptu made-up story or play. Scott spent a long, long time fixing a package for his father one day. It consisted of wadded up green tissue paper wrapped with white paper and taped together within an inch of its life. I alerted my husband by phone to show his appreciation because Scott had worked so very hard on his "present."

Vary the routine. Vary the pre-dinner routine. If the children seem especially tired, give them a soothing bath (or shower if they always take baths). If they always watch cartoons before dinner, load them in the stroller or wagon and go for a walk. If their tummies won't last until dinner is ready, grab a hamburger at McDonald's. A change of pace can eliminate boredom and revive tired bodies.

THINGS TO DO AWAY FROM HOME

Go somewhere. Sometimes the best solution is just to go somewhere. The hours seem to drag less if you are on the move. Take the children to the park, go visit a friend, or find some other activity that will keep them entertained without wearing them out.

Story hours. Check your local library for the time of their story hour for preschoolers.

Hire help. Hire a high-school girl to come in after school and watch the children for a couple of hours. With the help of a capable girl, I often used the time between 3:30 and 5:00 to run errands.

Swap baby-sitting. Arrange to swap baby-sitting with a friend once a week during the pre-dinner hour.

Meet Daddy at work. Catch a bus (or drive) and go meet Daddy when he gets off work.

With a little pre-planning on your part, you can keep the pre-dinner hours from becoming a free-for-all. And you'll all be in better spirits when Dad comes home.

Note
1. Margaret Self, ed., *Now What Can We Do?* (Ventura, CA: Regal Books, 1977), p. 47.

Chapter 13

Where shall we go this weekend?

A discussion about death came up at the dinner table one night and Scott said, "We wouldn't want to die. We want to be a family."

Some of the happiest memories you and your children will have through the years will be of the things you did together as a family. The times when Dad sets aside the many repair jobs every house demands, Mom forgets about the dishes and the laundry, and the whole family packs up and goes somewhere together. Or maybe you simply stay home and enjoy some treasured family activity. These are the times when we marvel at the wonders of God's creation, get to know each other better, learn to do new things. They are times of loving and growing and caring.

There are many things you can do together as a family. Some are more suitable for older children. But there are lots of activities toddlers can enjoy as well. I have been dismayed to note how many activities suggested in books and magazines are for children *over* the age of three. One author even went so far as to say that there really isn't much you can do with children under three. I disagree. Without some challenges to their environment and yours, you end up simply doing "maintenance care," as a friend calls it (maintaining the clean diaper supply, providing food for them to eat, cleaning up after them). If you plan your activities according to children's needs and abilities, even your youngest child can have a good time.

GENERAL GUIDELINES

Plan outings the *children* will enjoy (rather than adult-oriented ones), and you'll all have a better time. The less structure the better for little ones. Remember that their attention span is short. Don't expect them to stand or sit still for long periods of time. A friend and I took our five preschoolers to the Museum of Science and Industry. We covered the entire building at lightning speed, but we all had a great time. The children absorbed what they could understand and moved on when something was over their heads.

Prepare the children ahead of time for special trips. If you will be visiting a museum or other hands-off place, let them know what is expected of them.

Like metal to a magnet, children are drawn to restrooms and drinking fountains. Even if they have pottied and drunk moments before, the intrigue is irresistible. Allow plenty of time for these necessities in your schedule.

Children are also drawn to dirt (you've noticed!). Pack a wet washcloth in a plastic bag and stash it in your purse for last-minute cleanups. Be sure also to pack plenty of diapers, extra clothes, and bottles for the baby.

Obtain a guidebook to attractions in your area and study it for ideas. If there is a book listing specifically child-oriented places to visit, so much the better. Also watch your local newspaper (calendar or amusement section) for places and events to visit.

TRAVELING BY CAR/TRAIN/BUS/PLANE

Confining small children to an automobile for longer than 15 minutes can test your fortitude. Some children travel quite well, others are restless and cranky in a very short time. Differences in personalities and attention spans will affect how well they cope.

Here are some suggestions which can help relieve some of the tension:

● Don't give trips too big a build-up ahead of time. Otherwise the children may already be so keyed up they have a hard time settling down.

● Fill a drawstring bag with new (or new to them) toys to play with, especially selected for the trip, rather than ones they may already be tired of. Work out a swap with a friend—borrow some toys her child is not using at the moment and return them after the trip.

● For long car trips, take along a small trike or two to help the children work off energy at rest stops. Keep your eyes open for parks along the way where your little ones can stretch their legs.

● Don't make a big deal out of a limited amount of tussling. ("He's touching me! Tell him to leave me alone!") If you don't let it get to *you*, it will be less of a problem for everyone.

● Fill old Band-Aid boxes with little trinkets (old jewelry, simple card games, balloons, etc.).

● Take longer to get there than you might have planned. Periodic rest stops and even an overnight stay at an inexpensive motel (with a swimming pool or playground) will keep tempers from flaring.

● When traveling by airplane, ask to be allowed to board the plane first. Preference is usually given to families with young children. Also you might request seating in the front row of economy class (unless you are fortunate enough to travel first class). The front row usually has more leg room and may even have a wall attachment for a small bassinet for the baby.

● On airplane flights, be sure to take a bottle for babies and gum for toddlers. The air pressure sometimes affects their ears and is very painful. My daughter screamed for about an hour one time on a short flight because I had failed to bring a bottle on board the plane. When I finally discovered what was wrong, I felt like the world's worst mother.

● Be sure to take along a change of clothes for the children, even on short trips. Even if your child is past the wetting stage, food and drinks can be spilled and clothes ruined.

● Realize that traveling with small children is work. There's no other word for it. But that doesn't mean you can't all have a good time.

EATING IN RESTAURANTS

Unless you are an inveterate picnicker, there will probably be a number of restaurant stops on your outings. I think it is important for children to learn proper restaurant manners along with everything else they learn. But a table or booth full of hungry kids is no picnic! To keep them from bouncing off the walls until the food arrives, try these suggestions:

● Keep a supply of pens or pencils in your purse and let them draw on paper napkins and placemats. This is a good time for older preschoolers to practice printing their name.

● If the restaurant uses cloth napkins, show the children how to make things with the napkins: fold into a hat, fashion into an ice cream cone or other object, wrap around your hand and make a hand puppet.

● Play "I see" and take turns naming objects or colors they see around the room.

● Ask the waitress for crackers to stave off hunger pangs.

● Let one adult order the food and the other keep the children outdoors for a while. This is good especially if you have been traveling for some distance. It gives the children a chance to stretch their legs and run off some of their energy.

● Pray that the waitress comes quickly.

There are many things you can do as a family that cost nothing—or very little—yet provide enjoyment for all. Some things will be planned, some spontaneous. Occasionally you may want to include someone else in your plans—one of your child's friends, a relative, a neighbor. Here are some suggestions to supplement your own ideas.

THINGS TO DO AT HOME

● *Involve the children in whatever you are doing.* If you are cooking, let the children stir, operate the beater (with careful supervision), grate and cut (with a dull knife). When my husband is doing some repair job, he gives the children some pieces of lumber, nails and a hammer and lets them work with him. They have spent hours arranging pieces of lumber to make a "house." Children can learn to weed, rake leaves, shovel snow, or do other small projects. Let it be a game for them and one which they can leave when they tire of it. The older ones, however, also need to learn to put things away when they are finished with them. If you are painting outdoors, give the children brushes and a bucket of water. Let them "paint" the sidewalk or side of the garage.

● *Include the children in your own hobbies and interests.* A school teacher friend of ours enjoys model trains. His daughter has fun going with him to the hobby shop to see the various kinds of trains. When he grades papers at night, he lets his daughter do her "office work" nearby with bits of paper. He and his wife also enjoy looking at old houses. Their four-year-old now says, "Look at that old house, Mommy," when she spots one. Children can learn by participating in whatever interests us.

● *Sing together.* Children love to sing and to share their favorite songs from nursery school and Sunday School. Learn their songs so you can sing with them. And teach them some of your own.

● *Pray together.* At mealtime we take turns praying and we often hold hands. Besides fostering togetherness, holding hands helps keep little fingers from poking someone or sneaking a bite to eat. Pray together at bedtime or any other time. Sometimes children share things in their prayers that they may not have mentioned to their parents.

● *Light a fire in the fireplace and toast marshmallows.* Tell the children stories about when they were born or things they did when they were younger. Children love to hear about themselves and will ask for those stories over and over.

Throw in a story or two about your own childhood also. One of the ways a child really gets to know you is by knowing about your past. My husband has always felt that he did not really know his mother because she seldom talked about herself (she came from Scotland). He was the fifth of six children, and apparently the stories about her life had all been told several times by the time he came along.

● *Go through the children's baby albums or albums of pictures taken on a special trip or event* (dedication, birthday, etc.). At one of our daughter's birthday parties we showed the children a home movie of her very first birthday party. Of course, some of the children at the party were also in the movie, which made it especially fun for us all.

● *Plant a small garden.* The whole family can help spade up the ground, work in the fertilizer, plant the seeds and set up the row markers. A small fence may be necessary to remind the children where not to walk. You will all enjoy watching the first leaves appear and later harvesting the crop.

● *See* Good Times for Your Family *by Wayne E. Rickerson (Regal Books) for more ideas* of things your family can do to build communication, teach Christian values and learn Bible truths.

THINGS TO DO IN YOUR COMMUNITY

● *What does your church offer that preschoolers can participate in with you?* One of the happiest memories I have is of a pancake breakfast our church's high-school department sponsored several months ago. The children are too young to sit through sermons, films and other church programs. But a pancake breakfast is something we can all enjoy.

During the meal our youth minister and a couple of college boys played the guitar and sang for us. One of our three-year-olds asked if they would sing "Jesus Loves Me," which they did. When the other boy requested "Away in a Manger" they came over to our table and sang his request especially for him. It meant a great deal to me that they were willing to honor the requests of two very young boys.

● I read somewhere recently that 30 percent of the people who *visit shopping malls* do so for the diversion, not because they have anything to buy. That probably holds true in our household as well. We've made our local mall a family outing on more than one occasion. Our two-level mall has escalators, an elevator and a pet shop. When our browsing and riding are over, we can stop at the food area for an ice cream cone.

● *Take a walk.* Play "I spy" or "I see." "I see" a yellow butterfly (a blue bird, a green door). Look for different kinds of windows (round, rectangular, square, stained glass).

On your walk pick up brightly colored leaves. (We did that one Thanksgiving and glued the leaves to place cards for our Thanksgiving dinner table.) Or pick up rocks and compare their colors. When you get home, dip them in water and watch the colors change. If the children have "house fever" during a rainstorm, put on boots and raincoats, take your umbrella and go for a walk. Children love walking in the puddles.

After Christmas dinner one year we decided to take a walk around our neighborhood. We must have walked for two or three hours, just leisurely strolling and looking at homes and yards. We discovered some new homes just being built a few blocks over and peeked in the windows. Whenever a little one got tired, there was always an adult to carry him (the grandparents were with us also). It was one of the most enjoyable (and economical) family outings we've had.

• *Visit a museum or art gallery.* A science museum with stuffed birds and animals is ideal for young children. But don't shy away from art museums either. To introduce your children to art, suggests one mother, stop first at the museum gift shop and select one or more post cards that are reproductions of paintings or sculpture in the museum. Let the child look for the original that matches the picture on the card. The card then becomes his souvenir to take home.

See if the museum has a children's guide. When my husband and I visited the J. Paul Getty Museum in Malibu, California recently, we picked up a copy of the children's guide. It told what to look for in certain paintings—things that would interest children. We found it helpful for us as adults, even though our children were not with us at the time.

• *Take a tour of a factory, bakery, lumber mill, or other place where you can watch things being made.* Talk about how the item is made, who buys it, where it is sold. If it's edible, try a sample.

• *Take a trip to the beach.* Even when it's cold, bundle up and let the kids run and scream to their hearts' delight. There's nothing quite as much fun for children as building sand castles or covering Daddy with sand. Be sure to take along shovels and pails for digging.

When I was a child growing up in Washington, we often found beautiful agates at the beach. I learned early to watch where my feet were going to discover beautiful treasures.

● *Visit ethnic celebrations* (Greek, Mexican-American, Japanese, etc.) to help your children learn about other cultures. Exposure to the costumes, folk dances, music and food can be fun for the whole family.

● *Make arrangements for your family to visit a convalescent hospital.* Elderly people confined to such places seldom see children and are delighted with a visit, even from children they do not know. Perhaps your family could put on a short program—singing, reading a few verses from the Bible, perhaps showing some slides of a scenic spot you visited.

● *Take a tour of your neighborhood, by car or on foot, and see what you can discover and learn.* Look at and name the flowers in the florist's window. (You might want to buy a few to take home.) Let the children watch the revolving clothing rack at the dry cleaning establishment. Visit the post office and watch the mail trucks. Watch the cars going through a car wash. If there is a military installation such as a National Guard Armory ask permission to watch the men drilling. Other stops could include the library, police station, bus terminal, etc. If a particular industry is located in your town, see if a visit to the factory or warehouse is possible.

● *Visit a marina and watch the boats go in and out of the harbor.* Notice the large yachts, small tugboats, brightly colored sails on the sailboats. You may want to take a short cruise.

● *Visit an airport and watch take-offs and landings.* Notice the varied size from the small commuter planes to the large commercial aircraft. Point out the control tower and the refueling procedures and watch the baggage come off the conveyor.

● *Attend community celebrations such as parades, picnics, art exhibits and craft shows.* If a particular artisan is demonstrating his craft, the children will enjoy learning how something is made.

● *Attend an outdoor concert where little ones have some freedom of movement.* Older preschoolers may be able to sit through an indoor concert. We once took Shana (who was about five) to a concert featuring explanation and demonstration of a variety of different instruments. Since it was held in a school gymnasium, she was free to move about on the bleachers if she got restless. Her attention was much better than I had expected.

● *Take a bus ride to a part of the city you don't normally visit.* Consult a visitor's guide for places of interest to see and do, or simply take a self-guided walking tour.

SHORT TRIPS

● *If Daddy is attending a convention, go with him.* Ask at the hotel what facilities are available for children (parks, children's museums, etc.). When Daddy is not attending meetings, he will be able to spend time with his family.

● *Check your denominational and other Christian camps in your area for programs designed for families.* In our area Forest Home Christian Conference Center sponsors a Memorial Day weekend conference for families. Activities for the whole family are provided as well as some just for junior age through adults in the evening (with baby-sitting provided for younger children).

● *Buy or rent a tent and go camping.* Exploring God's creation is a relaxing way to get away from the activities of everyday life. (It can also be a lot of work. Simplify cooking and other chores as much as possible.) Gather leaves, nuts, rocks, shells and thank God with your children for the wonderful world He has given us. Give each child a small pail or other container to carry his treasures home in.

● *Take a short train ride to a neighboring city or scenic attraction.* An hour or two on the train is sufficient to give the whole family a refreshing change of pace.

● *If you live in an urban area, locate orchards that allow families to pick fruit during harvest time.* Or visit a large Farmers' Market in your own city. The sights and smells of a large market are dazzling. See how many of the fruits and vegetables the children can name. If there is a meat market, show them the different kinds of fish, fowl and meat. Bring home some of the fresh food to eat.

• *If you live in a rural area, take a trip to the big city.* Locate ahead of time places of special interest to childen. Perhaps there is a hotel with a view of the city from the top floor. Ride a bus or other public transportation. Walk the downtown area at Christmas time and look at all the lights and decorations in the department stores.

There is a wide variety of resource books to give you ideas. Perhaps two of the best are *The Mother's Almanac* by Marguerite Kelly and Elia Parsons and *The Father's Almanac* by S. Adams Sullivan (both published by Doubleday).

CHAPTER 14

This too shall pass

It was 6:30 P.M. on Thanksgiving eve. Eight people were coming for dinner the next day and not one item of food had been prepared. Not that I'm a poor planner. It's just that my four-year-old daughter and two-year-old twin boys had, as usual, demanded every moment of my time.

It was the same day a friend had called urging me to turn on the TV. A mother of 10 (or some incredible number) was being interviewed and my friend thought I might pick up some home management techniques.

What does a woman who has time to be on TV know about what I'm going through, I grumbled. Her kids are probably all in college. I turned on the TV to oblige my friend, but the noise level at our house prevented my hearing it. It was just as well.

"Unless I have some time to cook," I declared to my just-home-from-work husband, "there will be no Thanksgiving." And my husband, wonderful man that he is, took the three children and promptly did a disappearing act.

After they left, I needed a few moments to pull myself together before attacking the kitchen. Grabbing the first pillow I came to I began beating out my frustrations on my son's bed. "I will never, never, never write pious platitudes about how to raise kids," I promised myself and the Lord.

What parents of preschoolers need, I decided, are words of

encouragement written *by* parents who are right in the thick of the battle.

Well, I have written this book in the thick of the battle. And the mothers and fathers who have contributed to this book are right in there pitching with *their* families of preschoolers. I can't give you a sure cure for colic, the perfect plan for potty training, or an unbeatable way to keep the mealtime noise level below the 12 decibel mark. Every child is different. So is every parent. What I have tried to do is to suggest a variety of answers to specific problems—a sort of potpourri of ideas that have worked for us and for other parents. From those ideas you can pick and choose.

To conclude this book I want to suggest some principles of child-rearing that have helped me through the most difficult days.

PRINCIPLE #1

The first principle is that *the rewards and results of child-rearing are long-term*. Turning a baby into a civilized human being is not done overnight. When my children turned two I would dearly have loved it if instant obedience had been the order of the day. Six months later they finally began to get the message that when Mother calls she means come, not run in the other direction. Consistent discipline brings results, but it may take two months, six months, or maybe even years.

A few rewards, of course, are instantaneous. Like the sticky kiss planted firmly, and unexpectedly, on my cheek after I have just scolded my two-year-old for depositing his sucker on brother's hair. Or my four-year-old who tells me at bedtime—without any prompting—"I'm the one who broke the vase, Mommy. I'm sorry." Or my now six-year-old daughter who sees me resting in the afternoon and says sweetly, "Do you need pieces and quiet, Mommy?" and quietly closes the door so I can sleep. But many, many things take months and even years before the results of our efforts are known.

If we expect our children to behave in certain ways before they are capable of such behavior, we place unhealthy pressures on them. Then, if they never quite measure up to our expectations, we wrongly conclude that either we or they are failures. Children deserve a little time to prove themselves.

PRINCIPLE #2

Do not make yourself a slave to other people's ideas on how to raise children is the second principle. Get together a group of mothers and there will be as many sure-fire suggestions on how to stop temper tantrums as there are mothers present. And the Dads would probably have another set of their own. The suggestions of others can be extremely helpful at times, but they must be tempered with your own good sense and intuition.

Some time ago I participated in a discussion group consisting of mothers of preschoolers. During the discussion we came to the conclusion that by the time the first child is about two years old, the child's mother has developed a fair amount of self-confidence in her role. Up until that time she may be frustrated and confused. Her mother tells her one thing. Her pediatrician tells her another. And her friends tell her something else.

It may take a couple of years, but gradually you come to realize that you and you alone usually know what is best for your child. I do not mean to imply that we then shut out all outside suggestions. Quite the contrary. I am grateful for the relative who gave us the final push, when Scott was ill, to call the doctor one more time and get him to the emergency room. But you will find it easier after the first couple of years to sift and sort through the many suggestions about child-rearing that come your way. Gradually you and your husband will develop more and more confidence in your growing ability to know what is best for your child.

A friend tells me she breast-fed one of her children for four-and-a-half years. The other two weaned themselves at eight months and one year respectively, but one of the children hung on for an unusually long time. I don't need to describe for you the looks and comments she received from neighbors and relatives. And my friend used to ask herself in bewilderment, "Why am I doing this?" Yet something inside her told her it was right.

When the child was five my friend learned that her daughter

was hyperactive. The doctor told her that nursing was the child's way of calming herself when she felt herself getting out of control.

"If you had not nursed her," the doctor said, "you would have her in therapy today."

Trust yourself. Do not let well-meaning friends and relatives pressure you into doing things you do not really feel are right for your child. Nine times out of ten your own intuition will be right.

PRINCIPLE #3

The third principle is that *parenting is a team effort*. I do not believe that one set of parents can do everything for and be everything to any given child. When children are dedicated or baptized in our church, the congregation is asked to pledge right along with the parents that they will help the children grow in the nurture and admonition of the Lord.

Parents are the most important people in any child's life. But they are not the only people. Grandparents can teach their grandchildren things that perhaps the parents don't have time to teach them. Christian grandparents can also reinforce the beliefs and values being taught by their children. The church and Sunday School are another source of help. Who of us who were raised in the church has not had a Sunday School teacher or a pastor who especially influenced our lives? No doubt you can think of someone in your life who taught you something, encouraged or influenced you as no other person was able to do.

Do not be afraid to share your children with others. And don't feel guilty because someone else does something for your child that you did not or could not do. It's all part of the team effort.

Parenting is also a team effort because as Christian parents God is at work in and through us. It is from Him we receive guidance. It is through His power we are able to guide our children into a personal knowledge of His Son. The spiritual guidance of children is by far the most important aspect of our parenting. If we have accepted Jesus Christ as Lord and Saviour of our lives, we have the assurance that He will never leave us nor forsake us in parenting or in anything else we do.

He has not left us in limbo. Rather He has provided us with all the resources we need. In His Word we find the means for our own spiritual growth, without which we can never hope to influence our children for Christ. He has also given us a wealth of books and classes, seminars and conferences on parenting to help us with the practical outworking of our jobs—resources generations before us never had. True, much that is offered from the field of psychology and elsewhere is of little value, even contrary to the teachings of Scripture. But God also gives us the spirit of discernment to determine what we can use and what we cannot. *True* psychology is absolutely biblical, for it stems from the One who created our mind and knows how it works far better than we.

Our children are really not ours at all, they are God's. He has simply loaned them to us for a time, to teach and to train, to enjoy and to love. And then we must set them free to serve Him in whatever way they choose. All the while He is there to guide us, to rejoice with us when they do right, to wipe our tears when they choose the wrong. In joy and in sorrow, in sickness and in health, He is always there.

I'm so glad I'm a part of that team.

PRINCIPLE #4

The fourth principle is simple—but profound—*this too shall pass*. It was a beautiful sunny fall day and the kids were in reasonably good moods. We spent most of the morning working in the backyard. I swept a load of leaves across the patio—and Scott swept them back. Occasionally a leaf made it into the trash can.

During the day all of the BMs destined for the toilet—made it (with none left over for the floor or step stool).

Only one glass of milk was spilled at lunch (on the picnic table, who cares?).

Nobody threw up on the brocade couch or dumped yogurt on the carpet.

I even broke up laughing in the middle of scolding No. 2 son because he was just too funny to believe.

All told it was one of our better days. When the bad times

come, I can look back on days like that and remember that this too shall pass. God never gives us more than we can handle.

"Your house sure is clean," a friend said the other day. "I remember when you could barely shovel through."

During the first few years with our children, it seemed like the house was always a disaster. If I managed to get it straightened, it never stayed that way for more than 30 seconds. And most of the time I was too tired to do much more than clear a path through. I didn't like living like that. But time and energy did not permit much else.

Things have changed. My children are older and life is not nearly as harried at our house as it was when they were one and three. If you despair of ever being able to clear through the rubble, this too shall pass.

When the boys were learning to talk, they used to sit at the dinner table, point to what they wanted, and scream. No amount of shushing would quiet them because it was the only way they knew how to communicate. They were not yet able to put their thoughts into words. They could only point and scream. Needless to say, mealtime was a deafening affair. It seemed like it lasted an eternity. In retrospect I discovered that it only lasted about six weeks. When they were able to verbalize, they no longer needed to scream.

Remember your toddler sitting in her high chair carefully and meticulously pushing pieces of food over the edge of the tray when you weren't watching? So much for a clean floor. But the next thing you know, she's eating properly with a fork and spoon.

And we thought they'd never be potty trained. They'd probably go through life with a diaper pail stashed in the bathroom. But how many junior highers have you met who haven't licked the problem? Toilet training, like everything else, will pass with time.

It seemed like the children would never learn to be quiet and reverent during prayer time before meals. Someone was always snickering, poking, sneaking something to eat. Were they never going to learn reverence and respect? What were we doing wrong? Then one day we sat down to pray and the room was as still as a mouse. I thought they'd never learn . . . but they did.

We rejoice when the problems pass. But many of the joys pass also. I look at my long-legged daughter trotting off to first grade and it seems like only yesterday her diapered bottom was toddling around our house.

In the midst of an overload of diapers, formula, sleepless nights and all the rest, people used to say, "Oh, they grow up so fast. Enjoy them while you can." To an overworked mother too tired to stand on her feet it seemed like idle chatter. Just a year or two further down the road, however, and now I understand how quickly time really does pass.

My six-year-old is not a baby any more and neither are her brothers. She's a young lady marching headlong toward womanhood. In retrospect, the preschool years don't last very long at all.

For months the boys called fire engines and sirens "gwuy gwuy." We never did figure out how they came up with that particular sound. But for us it was one of those "cute" things toddlers do and say. Then one day Scott looked at a picture of a fire engine and said, "Gwuy gwuy." "No," said Reed, "it's a fire engine." And that was the end of an era.

Even things I have written about my children in this book have changed with the passage of only a few months or a year. My strong-willed two-year-old has become a cooperative, enjoyable four-year-old. The three-year-old who had trouble verbalizing his ideas now delights and amazes us with some of the things he says. The toddler who seldom let me out of her sight now marches off to school as independent as the next one (well, almost).

Be they good or bad, enjoyable or not so, the preschool years pass ever so quickly. Ponder the joys and savor the things your preschoolers do and say. Before long, this too shall pass.

In some ways, these are the easy times. It takes a lot of work to care for young children. But the strain is largely physical. In years to come, the physical will be replaced by the emotional.

"It used to be," says a friend with three teenagers, "that my day ended at 8:00 when the children were in bed. Now it's just beginning." Soon the years come when, by what used to be bedtime, the children are out on dates, at parties or somewhere else. The drain on your energy is replaced by new challenges to your emotions.

PRINCIPLE #5

The fifth principle is the one that gives meaning and purpose to both the good days and the bad: *The trials of parenthood are designed by God to make us more like Christ.*

"God allows problems, irritations and responsibilities to come into our lives," wrote our minister in his sermon notes one Sunday, "so that we are motivated to search out His Word and develop the full potential which He put within our lives." He continued:

> God knows that, left to ourselves, many of us would only develop a small portion of the aptitudes, abilities and capacities which He has put within us. To the degree that we didn't develop the rest, we would experience boredom in our lives with all its negative results. Therefore, in order to direct and motivate us in developing the rest, God chooses to bring into our lives certain problems, irritations and responsibilities.

If your preschoolers push you to the very limits of your cope-ability, know that it is for a reason. (Situations that have purpose are easier to bear.) God has chosen the situation you are in to help you (and me) develop and grow.* Jesus Christ was pushed to the limits of His humanness, too, and the end result was a better view of His divinity.

If I compare yesterday to today, I don't think I've made much progress. But if I look back over a year or two, I find that I really have grown, at least in some areas. I also find that I have a lot more growing to do.

The preschool years are not easy. But I wouldn't trade them. For in them God is forging a new me.

* My husband read this and said he will read it back to me some afternoon when he comes home from work. Being reminded of what you've said by those you love is one of the tests of growth!